MUKUNDA-MĀLĀ-STOTRA

BOOKS by
His Divine Grace A. C. Bhaktivedanta
Swami Prabhupāda

Bhagavad-gītā As It Is
Śrīmad-Bhāgavatam (18 vols.; with disciples)
Śrī Caitanya-caritāmṛta (9 volumes)
The Nectar of Devotion
Kṛṣṇa, the Supreme Personality of Godhead
Teachings of Lord Caitanya
Śrī Īśopaniṣad
The Nectar of Instruction
Easy Journey to Other Planets
Kṛṣṇa Consciousness: The Topmost Yoga System
Perfect Questions, Perfect Answers
Teachings of Lord Kapila, the Son of Devahūti
Transcendental Teachings of Prahlāda Mahārāja
Dialectic Spiritualism—A Vedic View of Western Philosophy
Teachings of Queen Kuntī
Kṛṣṇa, the Reservoir of Pleasure
The Science of Self-Realization
Search for Liberation
Life Comes from Life
The Path of Yoga
Beyond Birth and Death
On the Way to Kṛṣṇa
Rāja-vidyā: The King of Knowledge
Elevation to Kṛṣṇa Consciousness
Kṛṣṇa Consciousness: The Matchless Gift
The Nārada-bhakti-sūtra (with disciples)
The Mukunda-mālā-stotra (with disciples)
The Journey of Self-Discovery
The Quest for Enlightenment
The Laws of Nature: An Infallible Justice
A Second Chance
Renunciation Through Wisdom
The Perfection of Yoga
Message of Godhead
Civilization and Transcendence
Geetār-gān (Bengali)
Bhakti-ratna-boli (Bengali)
Back to Godhead magazine (founder)

A complete catalog is available upon request.

The Bhaktivedanta Book Trust
3764 Watseka Avenue
Los Angeles, California 90034

E-mail: letters@harekrishna.com
Telephone: 1-800-927-4152
http://www.harekrishna.com/~ara/

MUKUNDA-MĀLĀ-STOTRA

THE PRAYERS OF KING KULAŚEKHARA

HIS DIVINE GRACE
A. C. BHAKTIVEDANTA SWAMI PRABHUPĀDA
Founder/*Ācārya* of the
International Society for Krishna Consciousness
And His Disciples

THE BHAKTIVEDANTA BOOK TRUST
Los Angeles • London • Stockholm • Bombay • Sydney • Hong Kong

THE COVER: When King Kulaśekhara saw the breathtaking beauty of Lord Kṛṣṇa in ecstatic trance, he lost all desire to rule his vast kindom. Later he wrote, "My mind cannot turn from Śrī Kṛṣṇa's lotus feet, even for a moment. So let my dear ones and other relatives criticize me, my superiors accept or reject me as they like, the common people spread evil gossip about me, and my family's reputation be sullied. For a madman like me, it is honor enough to feel this flood of love of Godhead, which brings such sweet emotions of attraction for my Lord." In the *Mukunda-mālā-stotra,* Kulaśekhara implores us to join him in such divine madness.

Readers interested in the subject matter of this book are invited by the International Society for Krishna Consciousness to correspond with its secretary at one of the following addresses:

International Society for Krishna Consciousness
3764 Watseka Avenue
Los Angeles, California 90034
USA
Telephone: (800) 927-4152

International Society for Krishna Consciousness
P.O. Box 324, Borehamwood
Herts. WD6 1NB
England
Telephone: 01-905 1244

International Society for Krishna Consciousness
P. O. Box 262
Botany
N.S.W. 2019
Australia

First printing, 1992: 2,000
Second printing, 1998: 2,000

Printed in the United States of America

Printed in the United States of America

Library of Congress Cataloging-in-Publication Data

Kulaśekhara, 9th cent.
[Mukundamālā. English & Sanskrit]
Mukunda-mālā-stotra : the prayers of King Kulaśekhara / A. C. Bhaktivedanta Swami Prabhupāda and Satsvarūpa Dāsa Goswami.
p. cm.
Includes index.
ISBN 0-89213-275-2
1. Krishna (Hindu deity)—Prayer-books and devotions—English.
2. Krishna (Hindu deity)—Prayer-books and devotions—Sanskrit.
3. Kulaśekhara, 9th cent. Mukundamālā. I. Bhaktivedanta Swami Prabhupāda, 1896–1977. II. Goswami, Satsvarūpa Dāsa, 1939– .
BL1220.2.K8713 1992
294.5'43—dc20 92-31102
CIP

Contents

Introduction

Of the many hundreds of poetic Sanskrit *stotras*—songs of glorification offered to the Supreme Lord, His devotees, and the holy places of His pastimes—King Kulaśekhara's *Mukunda-mālā-stotra* is one of the most perennially famous. Some say that its author conceived it as a garland (*mālā*) of verses offered for Lord Kṛṣṇa's pleasure. It has long been dear to Vaiṣṇavas of all schools, and our own spiritual master, Śrīla A. C. Bhaktivedanta Swami Prabhupāda, frequently enjoyed citing certain favorite stanzas from it.

King Kulaśekhara was part of the Śrī-sampradāya, the Vaiṣṇava school founded by Lord Viṣṇu's divine consort, Śrī. This school's most prominent representative, Rāmānuja Ācārya (eleventh century), built on the work of his predecessors Nātha Muni and Yāmuna Ācārya and established the systematic philosophy of Śrī Vaiṣṇavism. But these *ācāryas* came in an already old tradition, that of the ecstatic mystic poets called Ālvārs. The twelve Ālvārs appeared at various times in South India, in the area roughly corresponding to present-day Tamil Nadu. According to the tradition of the Śrī Vaiṣṇavas, the earliest Ālvārs lived more than five thousand years ago, at the start of the present age, Kali-yuga, while the most recent lived in the first millennium A.D.

The Ālvārs' Tamil poetry was collected in the *Tiruvāymoli,* revered by Śrī Vaiṣṇavas as their own vernacular *Veda.* On the strength of the *Tiruvāymoli's* devotional authority, the Śrī Vaiṣṇavas claim to follow Ubhaya-vedānta, the dual Vedānta philosophy founded on both Sanskrit and Tamil scripture. Some Ālvārs were atypical renunciants: the third, Āṇḍāl, was a woman, and three were involved in governing. Among these was the tenth Ālvār, Kulaśekhara Perumāl, who was a ruling king in the Cera dynasty of Malaināḍu, in what is now Kerala. Modern scholars say he may have lived during the ninth century A.D.

A traditional history of King Kulaśekhara states that once, as he slept in his palace quarters, he had a brilliant and distinct vision of Lord Kṛṣṇa. Upon awaking he fell into a devotional trance and failed to notice dawn breaking. The royal musicians and ministers came as usual to his door to wake him, but after waiting some time without hearing him respond, they reluctantly took the liberty of entering his room. The king came out of his trance and described his vision to them, and from that day on he no longer took much interest in ruling. He delegated most of his responsibilities to his ministers and dedicated himself to rendering devotional service to the Lord. After some years he abdicated the throne and went to Śrī Raṅgam, where he remained in the association of the Kṛṣṇa Deity of Raṅganātha and His many exalted devotees. At Śrī Raṅgam Kulaśekhara is said to have composed his two great works: the *Mukunda-mālā-stotra,* in Sanskrit; and 105 Tamil hymns, which were later incorporated into the *Tiruvāymoli* under the title *Perumāl-tirumoli.*

As the other Ālvārs do in their mystic expressions, in his *Perumāl-tirumoli* King Kulaśekhara emulates the roles of some of Lord Rāmacandra's and Lord Kṛṣṇa's intimate devotees: King Daśaratha; two of the Lord's mothers, Kauśalyā and Devakī; and some of the young cowherd women of Vṛndāvana. But Mahārāja Kulaśekhara expresses no pride in realizing such confidential devotional moods. On the contrary, with deep humility he repeatedly begs simply to be allowed to take his next births as a bird, fish, or flower in the place where Lord Kṛṣṇa enacts His pastimes, and in this way to enjoy the association of His devotees.

The *Mukunda-mālā-stotra,* although composed in elegant Sanskrit, is a simple expression of King Kulaśekhara's devotion to Kṛṣṇa and his eagerness to share his good fortune with everyone else. Being thus a very public work, it does not delve into intimate personal revelations or abstruse philosophical conundrums. Like most other works of the *stotra* genre, it aims less at presenting a plot than at vividly and honestly expressing the true feelings of a lover of God. With this much we the readers should be completely satisfied, because it is a rare opportunity for us when a devotee of King Kulaśekhara's stature opens his heart so freely—and in a way just appropriate for us, with all our imperfections, to appreciate.

About the Present Edition

Using a Sanskrit edition published by Śrīla Bhaktivinoda Ṭhākura in 1895, Śrīla Prabhupāda began translating the *Mukunda-mālā-stotra* in the late 1950's. But after completing six verses with commentary, he suspended it to work on the *Śrīmad-Bhāgavatam.* He never resumed it. Yet he clearly intended that the *Mukunda-mālā* be published, since he included it in the list of his other English books at the beginning of each of the three volumes of the *Bhāgavatam's* First Canto.

In 1989, the Governing Body Commission of the International Society for Krishna Consciousness requested Satsvarūpa dāsa Goswami to complete the *Mukunda-mālā-stotra.* One of Śrīla Prabhupāda's earliest disciples, Satsvarūpa Goswami had distinguished himself over the years as one of his most learned and literary followers. He had served as editor of *Back to Godhead* magazine—the Society's monthly journal—for most of the twenty-three years it had been published in the West, and had written many books already, most notably a six-volume biography of Śrīla Prabhupāda.

Satsvarūpa Goswami accepted the assignment and enlisted the help of Gopīparāṇadhana dāsa, the Bhaktivedanta Book Trust's Sanskrit editor, to translate the remaining forty-seven verses. Then he carefully prepared the purports, often quoting from Śrīla Prabhupāda's *Bhagavad-gītā, Śrīmad-Bhāgavatam,* and other works. The result is a book that we trust will be informative and enlivening to devotees, scholars, and laymen alike.

The Publishers

Editor's note: Citations from *Kṛṣṇa, the Supreme Personality of Godhead* are from 1996 edition. Citations from *The Nectar of Devotion* are from the 1982 edition.

MUKUNDA-MĀLĀ-STOTRA

TEXT 1*

श्रीवल्लभेति वरदेति दयापरेति
भक्तप्रियेति भवलुण्ठनकोविदेति ।
नाथेति नागशयनेति जगन्निवासेत्य्
आलापिनं प्रतिदिनं कुरु मां मुकुन्द ॥१॥

śrī-vallabheti vara-deti dayā-pareti
bhakta-priyeti bhava-luṇṭhana-kovideti
nātheti nāga-śayaneti jagan-nivāsety
ālāpinaṁ prati-dinaṁ kuru māṁ mukunda

śrī-vallabha—O beloved of Lakṣmī (the Supreme Lord's consort); *iti*—thus; *vara-da*—O bestower of benedictions; *iti*—thus; *dayā-para*—O causelessly merciful one; *iti*—thus; *bhakta-priya*—O You who are very dear to Your devotees; *iti*—thus; *bhava*—the repetition of birth and death; *luṇṭhana*—in plundering; *kovida*—O You who are expert; *iti*—thus; *nātha*—O Lord; *iti*—thus; *nāga-śayana*—O You who sleep on the serpent bed (of Ananta Śeṣa); *iti*—thus; *jagat-nivāsa*—O resort of the cosmos; *iti*—thus; *ālāpinam*—reciter; *prati-dinam*—every day; *kuru*—please make; *mām*—me; *mukunda*—O Mukunda.

TRANSLATION

O Mukunda, my Lord! Please let me become a constant reciter of Your names, addressing You as Śrī-vallabha ["He who is very dear to Lakṣmī"], Varada ["the bestower of benedictions"], Dayāpara ["He who is causelessly merciful"], Bhakta-priya ["He who is very dear to His devotees"], Bhava-luṇṭhana-kovida ["He who is expert at

---

*Translations and purports of the texts marked with an asterisk are by His Divine Grace A. C. Bhaktivedanta Swami Prabhupāda.

plundering the status quo of repeated birth and death"], Nātha ["the Supreme Lord"], Jagan-nivāsa ["the resort of the cosmos"], and Nāga-śayana ["the Lord who lies down on the serpent bed"].

PURPORT

A devotee of Godhead is he who glorifies the Personality of Godhead under the dictation of transcendental ecstasy. This ecstasy is a by-product of profound love for the Supreme, which is itself attained by the process of glorification. In this age of quarrel and fighting, the process of chanting and glorification recommended here by King Kulaśekhara is the only way to attain perfection.

Persons who are infected with the disease of material attachment and who suffer from the pangs of repeated birth and death cannot relish such recitation of the Lord's glories, just as a person suffering from jaundice cannot relish the taste of sugar candy. By nature sugar candy is as sweet as anything, but to a patient suffering from jaundice it tastes as bitter as anything. Still, sugar candy is the best medicine for jaundice. By regular treatment with doses of sugar candy, one can gradually get relief from the infection of jaundice, and when the patient is perfectly cured, the same sugar candy that tasted bitter to him regains its natural sweetness.

In the same way, glorification of the transcendental name, fame, attributes, pastimes, and entourage of the Personality of Godhead tastes bitter to those who are suffering from the infection of material consciousness, but it is very sweet to those who have recovered from this infection.

All mundane philosophers, religionists, and people in general, who are constantly suffering from the threefold miseries of material existence, can get freedom from all such troubles simply by chanting and glorifying the holy name, fame, and pastimes of the Supreme Lord. The Supreme Lord, the Absolute Truth, is all spirit, and therefore His name, fame, and pastimes are nondifferent from Him. All of them are identical. In other words, the holy name of the Lord is the Lord Himself, and this can be understood by realization. By chanting the holy names of the Lord, which are innumerable, one can actually associate with the Lord personally, and by such constant personal touch with the all-spiritual Lord, one will become spiritually self-realized. This process of self-realization is very suitable for the fallen souls of this age, when life is short and when people are slow in understanding the importance of spiritual realization, prone to be misled by false association and false spiritual masters, unfortunate in every respect, and continuously disturbed by innumerable material problems.

King Kulaśekhara, an ideal pure devotee of the Lord, shows us by his own realization how to offer prayers to the Lord. Since he is a *mahājana,* an authority in the line of devotional service, it is our prime duty to follow in his footsteps in order to achieve the highest devotional platform.

He first addresses the Lord as Śrī-vallabha, "He who is very dear to Lakṣmī." The Lord is the Supreme Personality of Godhead, and His consort, Lakṣmī, is a manifestation of His internal potency. By expanding His internal potency, the Lord enjoys His spiritual paraphernalia. In the highest spiritual realization, therefore, the Lord is not impersonal or void, as empiric philosophers conceive Him to be. Although He is not of the material world, He is much more than simply a negation of material variegatedness. He is positively the supreme enjoyer of spiritual variegatedness, of which Lakṣmī, the internal potency, is the fountainhead.

King Kulaśekhara next addresses the Lord as Varada, "the bestower of benedictions," because it is He alone who can deliver to us the actual substance—spiritual bliss. When we detach ourselves from His association, we are always in the midst of want and scarcity, but as soon as we get in touch with Him, our gradual endowment with all bliss begins. The first installment of this bliss is the clearance of the layer of dust that has accumulated in our hearts due to millions of years of material association. As soon as the dust of materialism is brushed aside, the clear mirror of the heart reflects the presence of the Lord. And as soon as we see Him we are automatically freed from all kinds of aspirations and frustrations. In that liberated state, everything is blissful in relation with the Lord, and one has no desires to fulfill and nothing to lament over. Thus, following the benediction, full spiritual bliss comes upon us, ushering in full knowledge, full life, and full satisfaction with our whole existence.

King Kulaśekhara next addresses the Lord as Dayāpara, "He who is causelessly merciful," because there is no one but the Lord who can be a causelessly merciful friend to us. He is therefore also called Dīna-bandhu, "the friend of the needy." Unfortunately, at times of need we seek our friends in the mundane world, not knowing that one needy man cannot help another. No mundane man is full in every respect; even a man possessing the greatest riches is himself needy if he is devoid of a relationship with the Lord. Everything is zero without the Lord, who is the digit that transforms zero into ten, two zeros into one hundred, three zeros into one thousand, and so on. Thus a "zero man" cannot become happy without the association of the Lord, the supreme "1."

The supreme "1" always wants to make our zero efforts valuable by His association, just as a loving father always wants an unhappy son to be in a prosperous position. A rebellious son, however, stubbornly refuses the cooperation of the loving father and thus suffers all sorts of miseries. The Lord, therefore, sends His bona fide representatives to all parts of the material creation, and sometimes He even comes Himself to reclaim His fallen sons. For this purpose He also exhibits the actual life in the transcendental world, which is characterized by relationships with Him in servitorship, friendship, parenthood, and consorthood. All relationships in the material world are but perverted reflections of these original relationships. In the mundane world we experience only the shadow of the reality, which exists in the spiritual world.

The all-merciful Lord is always mindful of our difficulties in the mundane world, and He is more eager to get us to return home, back to Godhead, than we are eager to go. He is by nature merciful toward us, despite our rebellious attitude. Even in our rebellious condition we get all our necessities from Him, such as food, air, light, water, warmth, and coolness. Yet because we have detached ourselves from Him, we simply mismanage this paternal property. The leaders of society, despite all their materialistic plans, are misleaders, for they have no plan to revive our lost relationship with the Lord. His bona fide devotees, however, try their utmost to broadcast the message of our transcendental relationship with Him. In this way the devotees work to remind the fallen souls of their actual position and to bring them back home, back to Godhead. Such stainless servants of Godhead are very dear to Him. They receive such special favor from the Lord for their compassionate work that they can even go back to Godhead in this very lifetime and not be forced to take another birth.

The Lord is therefore next addressed as Bhakta-priya, meaning "He who is very dear to His devotees" or "He who is very affectionate to His devotees." In the *Bhagavad-gītā* (9.29) the Lord very nicely describes His sublime and transcendental affection for His devotees. There the Lord declares that although He is undoubtedly equally kind to all living beings—because all of them are part and parcel of Him and are His spiritual sons—those who are especially attached to Him by love and affection, who regard nothing dearer than Him, are particularly dear to Him.

An example of such a pure devotee is Lord Jesus Christ, who agreed to be mercilessly crucified rather than give up preaching on behalf of God. He was never prepared to compromise on the issue of believing in God. Such a son of God cannot be other than dear to the Lord. Similarly, when Ṭhākura Haridāsa was told to give up chanting the holy name of God, he refused to do so, with the result that he was flogged in twenty-two marketplaces. And Prahlāda Mahārāja persisted in disagreeing with his father, the great atheist Hiraṇyakaśipu, and thus voluntarily accepted the cruelties his father inflicted upon him. These are some examples of renowned devotees of the Lord, and we should simply try to understand how dear such devotees are to Him.

The Lord has emphatically declared that no one can vanquish His devotee under any circumstances. A good example is Ambarīṣa Mahārāja. When the great mystic *yogī* Durvāsā deliberately attempted to take the life of Ambarīṣa, the Lord suitably punished Durvāsā, even though he was a poweful *yogī* who could approach all the demigods and even the Lord Himself.

Sometimes, even at the risk of having to cross many stumbling blocks, a devotee relinquishes all family connections and homely comforts for the Lord's service. Can the Lord forget all these sacrifices of His bona fide devotee? No, not even for a moment, for the relationship between the Lord and His devotee is reciprocal, as He clearly says in the *Bhagavad-gītā* (9.29): "Whoever renders service unto Me in devotion is a friend—is in Me—and I am also a friend to him."

A devotee is never as eager to see the Lord as he is to render service to Him. Yet the Lord does appear before His devotee, for He is just like an affectionate father, who is more eager to see his son than the son is to see him. There is no contradiction in such a quantitative difference in affection. Such a disparity exists in the original reality—between the Lord and His devotees—and is reflected here not only in the relations between parents and children in human society but even in the animal kingdom. Parental affection is exhibited even among lower animals because originally such affection in its fullness exists in God, the original father of all species of living beings. When a man kills an animal, God, the affectionate father, is perturbed and is pained at heart. Thus the slaughterer of the animal is suitably punished by the material energy, just as a murderer is punished by the government through police action.

By the mercy of the Lord, a devotee develops all the good qualities of God, for a devotee can never remain in the darkness of ignorance. A father is always anxious to impart knowledge and experience to his son, but the son can choose whether to accept such instructions. A submissive devotee becomes automatically enlightened in all the intricacies of knowledge because the Lord, from within, dissipates his ignorance with the self-illumined lamp of wisdom. If the Lord Himself instructs the devotee, how can he remain foolish like the mundane wranglers?

A father is naturally inclined to act for the good of his son, and when the father chastises his son, that chastisment is also mixed with affection. Similarly, all the living entities who have lost their place in paradise due to disobedience to the Supreme Father are put into the hands of the material energy to undergo a prison life of the threefold miseries. Yet the Supreme Father does not forget His rebellious sons. He creates scriptures for them like the *Vedas* and *Purāṇas* in order to revive their lost relationship with Him and awaken their divine consciousness. Intelligent persons take advantage of the knowledge contained in these scriptures and thus attain the highest perfection of life.

For His devotees, the Lord personally descends to this world to give them relief and save them from the insane acts of miscreants. It is foolish to try to impose the limits of an ordinary living being upon the unlimited potency of Godhead and obstinately maintain that the Supreme Lord cannot descend. To mitigate His devotees' material pangs, He descends as He is, yet He is not infected by material qualities.

As soon as a person agrees to surrender unto the Lord, the Lord takes complete charge of him. Satisfied with the activities of such a devotee, He gives him instruction from within, and thus the devotee becomes pure and advances on the path back to Godhead. The Lord is expert at guiding such a pure devotee, who is not at all anxious for material superiority. A pure devotee does not wish to possess material wealth, nor does he want to have a great following, nor does he desire a beautiful wife, for by the mercy of the Lord he knows the insignificance of material happiness. What he very sincerely desires at heart is to continue in the loving service of the Lord, even at the risk of taking birth again.

When a neophyte devotee deviates from the path of pure devotion and wants to simultaneously enjoy sense gratification and discharge devotional service, the all-merciful Lord very tactfully corrects the bewildered devotee by exhibiting before him the real nature of this material world. In the material world all relationships are actually mercenary but are covered by an illusory curtain of so-called love and affection. The so-called wives and husbands, parents and children, and masters and servants are all concerned with reciprocal material profit. As soon as the shroud of illusion is removed, the dead body of material so-called love and affection is at once manifest to the naked eye.

The Lord expertly removes the shroud of illusion for the neophyte devotee by depriving him of his material assets, and thus the devotee finds himself alone in the midst of his so-called relatives. In this helpless condition he experiences the awkwardness of his so-called relationships with his so-called wife and children. When a man is financially ruined, no one loves him, not even his wife or children. Such a poverty-stricken devotee more perfectly fixes his faith in the Lord, and the Lord then delivers him from the fate of frustration.

The entire cosmic creation is the Lord's expert arrangement for the delusion of the living beings who try to be false enjoyers. The living being's constitutional position is to be a servant of the Lord, but in the transcendental relationship the servant and the Lord are in one sense identical, for the Lord also serves the servant. The typical example is Śrī Kṛṣṇa's becoming the charioteer of His eternal servant Arjuna. Illusioned mundaners cannot understand the transcendental and reciprocal relationship between the Lord and His devotees, and therefore they want to lord it over material nature or cynically merge with the Absolute. Thus a living being forgets his constitutional position and wants to become either a lord or a mendicant, but such illusions are arrangements of Māyā, the Lord's illusory potency. A false life either as a lord or a mendicant meets with frustration until the living being comes to his senses and surrenders to the Lord as His eternal servant. Then the Lord liberates him and saves him from repeated birth and death. Thus the Lord is also addressed here as Bhava-luṇṭhana-kovida, "He who is expert at plundering the status quo of repeated birth and death." A sensible man understands his position as the eternal servant of the Lord and molds his life accordingly.

The Lord is also addressed as Nātha, the real Lord. One can attain the perfection of life only by serving the real Lord. The entire material atmosphere is surcharged with the false lordship of the living beings. The illusioned beings are all struggling for false lordship, and thus no one wants to serve. Everyone wants to be the lord, even though such lordship is conditional and temporary. A hardworking man thinks himself the lord of his family and estate, but actually he is a servant of desire and the employee of anger. Such service of the senses is neither pensionable nor terminable, for desire and anger are masters who are never to be satisfied. The more one serves them, the more service they exact, and as such the false overlordship continues until the day of annihilation. As a result, the foolish living being is pushed into degraded life and fails to recognize the Lord as the beneficiary of all activities, the ruler of the universe, and the friend of all entities. One who knows the real Lord is called a *brāhmaṇa,* but one who fails to know Him is called a *kṛpaṇa,* or number-one miser.

The Lord of the creative energy is called Ananta-śayana. The material energy is impregnated by the glance of this feature of the Lord and is then able to give birth to all organic and inorganic matter. Ananta-śayana sleeps on the bed of Śeṣa Nāga, who has a form like a serpent but is identical with the Lord. Because He sleeps on a serpent bed, the Lord is also knon as Nāga-śayana. By His spiritual energy Śeṣa Nāga sustains all the planetary globes upon His invisible hoods. Śeṣa Nāga is popularly known as Saṅkarṣaṇa, or "that which keeps balance by the law of magnetism." In the scientific world this feature of the Lord is referred to as the law of gravitation, but factually this law, which keeps all the planets floating in space, is one of the energies of the Lord. All the universes are born with the exhalation of the Lord as He lies on Śeṣa Nāga, and all of them are annihilated with His inhalation. Due to these functions of creation, maintenance, and annihilation, the Lord is celebrated by the name Jagan-nivāsa, indicating that He is the supreme resort of all the universes.

There are hundreds of thousands of other names of Lord Viṣṇu, and each one of them is as powerful as the Lord Himself. One can constantly chant any name of the Lord and thereby constantly associate with Him. There are no hard and fast rules for chanting His names. At any time and any stage of life one can freely chant them, but we are so unfortunate that we are too misled even to adopt this simple process. This is the way of Māyā, the Lord's misleading energy. However, one can avoid her ways simply by always remembering the lotus feet of the Lord. King Kulaśekhara prays for this facility from Mukunda, the Supreme Personality of Godhead.

TEXT 2*

जयतु जयतु देवो देवकीनन्दनोऽयं
जयतु जयतु कृष्णो वृष्णिवंशप्रदीपः ।
जयतु जयतु मेघश्यामलः कोमलाङ्गो
जयतु जयतु पृथ्वीभारनाशो मुकुन्दः ॥२॥

jayatu jayatu devo devakī-nandano 'yaṁ
jayatu jayatu kṛṣṇo vṛṣṇi-vaṁśa-pradīpaḥ
jayatu jayatu megha-śyāmalaḥ komalāṅgo
jayatu jayatu pṛthvī-bhāra-nāśo mukundaḥ

jayatu jayatu—all glories, all glories; *devaḥ*—to the Personality of Godhead; *devakī-nandanaḥ*—son of Devakī; *ayam*— this; *jayatu jayatu*—all glories, all glories; *kṛṣṇaḥ*—to Lord Kṛṣṇa; *vṛṣṇi*—of Vṛṣṇi (Lord Kṛṣṇa's forefather); *vaṁśa*—of the dynasty; *pradīpaḥ*—the beacon light; *jayatu jayatu*—all glories, all glories; *megha*—like a new cloud; *śyāmalaḥ*—who is blackish; *komala*—very soft; *aṅgaḥ*—whose body; *jayatu jayatu*—all glories, all glories; *pṛthvī*—the earth's; *bhāra*—of the burden; *nāśaḥ*—to the destroyer; *mukundaḥ*—Lord Śrī Kṛṣṇa.

TRANSLATION

All glories to this Personality of Godhead known as the son of Śrīmatī Devakīdevī! All glories to Lord Śrī Kṛṣṇa, the brilliant light of

the Vṛṣṇi dynasty! All glories to the Personality of Godhead, the hue of whose soft body resembles the blackish color of a new cloud! All glories to Lord Mukunda, who removes the burdens of the earth!

PURPORT

The theme of this verse is that the Supreme Truth is the Supreme Person. That the Lord's bodily texture and color are described indicates that He is a person, for the impersonal Brahman cannot have a body that is as soft as anything or whose hue is visualized. The Personality of Godhead appeared as the son of Vasudeva and Devakī because for a very long time they performed severe austerities to have the Supreme Lord as their son. Satisfied by their penance and determination, the Lord agreed to become their son.

From the description of the Lord's birth in the *Śrīmad-Bhāgavatam,* we learn that the Lord appeared before Vasudeva and Devakī as Nārāyaṇa, with four hands. But when they prayed to Him to conceal His divinity, the Lord became a small baby with two hands. In the *Bhagavad-gītā* (4.9) the Lord promises that one who simply understands the mysteries of His transcendental birth and deeds will be liberated from the clutches of Māyā and go back to Godhead. Therefore there is a gulf of difference between the birth of Kṛṣṇa and that of an ordinary child.

One may ask, Since the Supreme Lord is the original father of all living entities, how could a lady known as Devakī give birth to Him as her son? The answer is that Devakī no more gave birth to the Lord than the eastern horizon gives birth to the sun. The sun rises on the eastern horizon and sets below the western horizon, but actually the sun neither rises nor sets. The sun is always in its fixed position in the sky, but the earth is revolving, and due to the different positions of the revolving earth, the sun appears to be rising or setting. In the same way, the Lord always exists, but for His pastimes as a human being He seems to take birth like an ordinary child.

In His impersonal feature (Brahman) the Supreme Lord is everywhere, inside and outside: as the Supersoul (Paramātmā) He is inside everything, from the gigantic universal form down to the atoms and electrons; and as the Supreme Personality of Godhead (Bhagavān) He sustains everything with His energies. (We have already described this feature of the Lord in the purport to the previous verse, in connection with the name Jagan-nivāsa.) Therefore in each of His three features—Brahman, Paramātmā, and Bhagavān—the Lord is present everywhere in the material world. Yet He remains aloof, busy with His transcendental pastimes in His supreme abode.

Those with a poor fund of knowledge cannot accept the idea that the Lord appears in person on the face of the earth. Because they are not conversant with the intricacies of the Lord's transcendental position, whenever such people hear about the appearance of the Lord, they take Him to be either a superhuman being born with a material body or a historical personality worshiped as God under the influence of anthropomorphism or zoomorphism. But the Lord is not the plaything of such fools. He is what He is and does not agree to be a subject of their speculations, which perpetually lead them to conclude that His impersonal feature is supreme. The supreme feature of the Absolute Truth is personal—the Supreme Personality of Godhead. The impersonal Brahman is His effulgence, like the light diffused by a powerful fire. The fire burns in one place but diffuses its warmth and light all round, thus exhibiting its different energies. Similarly, by means of His variegated energies the Supreme Lord expands Himself in many ways.

Persons with a poor fund of knowledge are captivated by one part of His energy and therefore fail to penetrate into the original source of the energy. Whatever astounding energies we see manifest in this world, including atomic and nuclear energies, are all part and parcel of His material, or external, energy. Superior to this material energy, however, is the Lord's marginal energy, exhibited as the living being. Besides these energies, the Supreme Lord has another energy, which is known as the internal energy. The marginal energy can take shelter of either the internal energy or the external energy, but factually it belongs to the Lord's internal energy. The living beings are therefore infinitesimal samples of the Supreme Lord. Qualitatively the living being and the Supreme Lord are equal, but quantitatively they are different, for the Lord is unlimitedly potent whereas the living entities, being infinitesimal by nature, have limited potency.

Although the Lord is full with all energies and is thus self-sufficient, He enjoys transcendental pleasure by subordinating Himself to His unalloyed devotees. Some great devotees of the Lord cannot surpass the boundary of awe and veneration. But other devotees are in such an intense compact of love with the Lord that they forget His exalted position and regard themselves as His equals or even His superiors. These eternal associates of the Lord relate with Him in the higher statuses of friendship, parenthood, and consorthood. Devotees in a transcendental parental relationship with the Lord think of Him as their dependent child. They forget His exalted position and think that unless they properly feed Him He will fall victim to undernourishment and His health will deteriorate. Devotees in a conjugal relationship with the Lord rebuke Him to correct His behavior, and the Lord enjoys those rebukes more than the prayers of the *Vedas.* Ordinary devotees bound up by the formalities of Vedic rites cannot enter deep into such confidential loving service to the Lord, and thus their realization remains imperfect. Sometimes they even fall victim to the calamity of impersonalism.

Vasudeva and Devakī are confidential devotees of the Lord in the mood of parental love. Even greater than them are Nanda and Yaśodā, His foster parents in Vṛndāvana. The Lord takes great pleasure in being addressed as Devakī-nandana ("the son of Devakī"), Nanda-nandana ("the son of Nanda"), Yaśodā-nandana ("the son of Yaśodā"), Daśarathī ("the son of King Daśaratha"), Janakī-nātha ("the husband of Janakī"), and so on. The pleasure one gives the Lord by addressing Him by such names is many, many times greater than the pleasure He enjoys when He is addressed as the Supreme Father, the Greatest of the Great, Parameśvara, or anything of that nature, which indicate volumes of awe and veneration. Therefore the names King Kulaśekhara uses to glorify the Lord in this verse indicate his intimate transcendental relationship with the Lord.

As explained above, all the names of the Lord are as powerful as the Lord Himself, but one can experience different transcendental mellows by chanting His different transcendental names. For example, the *śāstra* (scripture) states that there are one thousand principal names of Lord Viṣṇu, the Personality of Godhead. But if a person utters the name Rāma only once, he gets the result of chanting one thousand names of Viṣṇu. And if somebody once chants the name Kṛṣṇa, he achieves the results obtained by chanting the name Rāma three times. In other words, uttering the name Kṛṣṇa once is equal to uttering three thousand other names of Viṣṇu.

Therefore King Kulaśekhara, knowing how pleased the Lord is to be addressed by a name indicating His transcendental relationships with His intimate devotees, and knowing also the potency of the name Kṛṣṇa, has chosen to glorify the Lord by addressing Him as Devakī-nandana and Kṛṣṇa. The king also addresses Him as Vṛṣṇi-vaṁśa-pradīpa ("the brilliant light in the Vṛṣṇi dynasty") because millions of generations of the Vṛṣṇi dynasty became sanctified by the Lord's appearance within it. The *śāstras* state that a family in which a pure devotee is born is sanctified for one hundred generations of ancestors and descendants. And the *śāstras* also state that every place within a radius of one hundred miles from where a devotee is born becomes sanctified. If a devotee can sanctify the place and family of his birth so extraordinarily, then what to speak of how completely the Lord can sanctify the place and family in which He chooses to take His birth.

The Lord's birth on the face of the earth is certainly very mysterious, and therefore it is difficult for ordinary men to believe in His birth. How can the all-powerful Lord take birth, seemingly like an ordinary man? The matter is explained in the *Bhagavad-gītā* (4.6), where the Lord says,

ajo 'pi sann avyayātmā bhūtānām īśvaro 'pi san
prakṛtiṁ svām adhiṣṭhāya sambhavāmy ātma-māyayā

"Although I am unborn and My transcendental body never deteriorates, and although I am the Lord of all living entities, by My transcendental potency I still appear in every millennium in My original transcendental form." From the *śāstra* we learn that the Lord takes birth not only in the family of human beings but also in the families of demigods, aquatics, animals, and so on. One may argue that an ordinary living being is eternal and unborn like the Lord and also takes birth in different species of life, and so there is no difference between the Lord and an ordinary living being. The difference is, however, that while an ordinary living being changes his body when he transmigrates from one species of life to another, the Lord never changes His body: He appears in His original body, without any change. Also, while there is a vast difference between the ordinary living entity and his body, there is no difference between the Lord and His body because He is pure spirit. In other words, there is no distinction between His body and His soul.

The word *avyayātmā* in the above verse from the *Bhagavad-gītā* clearly indicates that the Lord's body is not made of material elements. He is all spirit. Birth and death apply only to the material body. The body of the ordinary living being is made of material elements and is therefore subject to birth and death. But the Lord's body, being all spiritual and thus eternal, neither takes birth nor dies. Nor can the Lord be forced to take birth in some particular family due to His past deeds, as an ordinary living being is.

The Lord is the supreme controller of the material elements, and being endless and beginningless, He exists in all times—past, present, and future. And because He is absolute, He has nothing to do with vice and virtue. In other words, for Him "vices" and "virtues" are one and the same; otherwise the Lord would not be the Absolute Truth.

Since the Lord appears by His internal potency, His incarnations in different species of life are not the creation of the external potency, Māyā. Therefore those who think that the Supreme Lord appears in different forms by accepting a body made of material elements are wrong; their vision is imperfect because they do not understand how the Lord's internal potency works. The *Vedas* inquire, Where does the Supreme Lord stand? And the reply is immediately given: He stands on His internal potency. So the conclusion is that although the Lord may seem to assume a material body when He takes birth, like an ordinary being, in fact He does not, for there is no difference between Him and His body. Thus He remains the Absolute Truth in all His appearances in different species of life.

In other words, the living being and the Supreme Lord appear in this material world under different circumstances. One can easily understand these different circumstances if one understands how the Lord's different potencies work. As explained before, the Lord has three kinds of potency, namely, internal, marginal, and external. We have wide experience of the external, or material, potency, but we generally fail to inquire about the actions and reactions of the other two potencies. A simple example will help us understand how the Lord's potencies work. Consider three identities: God, a man, and a doll. The doll consists of material energy, the man is a combination of material and spiritual energy, and God consists wholly of spiritual energy. The doll is all matter, internally and externally. Man is externally matter but internally spirit. And God is all spirit, both internally and externally. As the doll is all matter, so God is all spirit. But the man is half spirit and half matter.

Thus the body of God and the body of a living being are differently constituted. Because the Lord's body is pure spirit, it never deteriorates, and therefore He is called *avyayātmā.* His body is absolute, beginningless, unborn, and eternal, while the material body of the living being is relative and therefore temporary—it undergoes birth and death. The living being himself, of course, is eternal, and if He so desires he can realize his eternality by merging into the body of the Absolute Truth or being reinstated in his constitutional position as an eternal servant of the Lord. If he does not do so, then his eternality is still maintained, but he remains ignorant of it.

The conclusion is that the Personality of Godhead appears in His original body, without any change, and this is made possible by His inconceivable potency. We should always remember that nothing is impossible for the omnipotent Lord. If He so desires, He can transform material energy into spiritual energy. Indeed, if he so desires He can bring the entire spiritual nature within the material nature, without the spiritual nature being affected by the material modes in any way.

The Lord's different potencies remain tightly under His control. In fact, the Lord actually has only one potency—namely, the internal potency—which He employs for different purposes. The situation is similar to how one uses electricity. The same electricity can be used for both heating and cooling. Such contradictory results are due to the expert handling of a technician. In the same way, by His supreme will the Lord employs His one internal potency to accomplish many different purposes. That is the information we get from the *śrutis* (*Śvetāśvatara Up.* 6.8): *parāsya śaktir vividhaiva śrūyate.*

The present verse of the *Mukunda-mālā-stotra* states that the color of the Lord's body is blackish, like that of a new cloud. Also, His body is very soft. Softness of the body is a sign of a great personality. The *śāstras* state that the following bodily features indicate a great personality: a reddish luster in seven places—the eyes, the palms, the soles, the palate, the lips, the tongue, and the nails; broadness in three places—the waist, the forehead, and the chest; shortness in three places—the neck, the thighs, and the genitals; deepness in three places—the voice, the intelligence, and the navel; highness in five places—the nose, the arms, the ears, the forehead, and the thighs; and fineness in five places—the skin, the hair on the head, the bodily hair, the teeth, and the fingertips. All these features are present in the body of the Lord.

The *Brahma-saṁhitā* confirms that the color the Lord's body is blackish, like that of a new cloud. But this blackish color is so beautiful that it surpasses the beauty of millions of Cupids. So this blackish color does not correspond to any blackish color in the material world.

Such descriptions of the Lord's body are not imaginary; rather, they are the statements of those who have seen the Lord with their supernatural vision. This supernatural vision is bestowed upon devotees like Brahmā and upon those who follow the footsteps of pure devotees like him. But upstarts and unbelievers cannot have any access to this transcendental vision, for they lack the required submission to the will of the Lord.

TEXT 3*

मुकुन्द मूर्ध्ना प्रणिपत्य याचे
भवन्तमेकान्तमियन्तमर्थम् ।
अविस्मृतिस्त्वच्चरणारविन्दे
भवे भवे मेऽस्तु भवत्प्रसादात् ॥३॥

mukunda mūrdhnā praṇipatya yāce
bhavantam ekāntam iyantam artham
avismṛtis tvac-caraṇāravinde
bhave bhave me 'stu bhavat-prasādāt

mukunda—O Lord Mukunda; *mūrdhnā*—with my head; *praṇipatya*—bowing down; *yāce*—I respectfully beg; *bhavantam*—from You; *ekāntam*—exclusively; *iyantam*—this much; *artham*—desire to be fulfilled; *avismṛtiḥ*—freedom from forgetfulness; *tvat*—Your; *caraṇa-aravinde*—at the lotus feet; *bhave bhave*—in each repeated birth; *me*—my; *astu*—let there be; *bhavat*—Your; *prasādāt*—by the mercy.

TRANSLATION

O Lord Mukunda! I bow down my head to Your Lordship and

respectfully ask You to fulfill this one desire of mine: that in each of my future births I will, by Your Lordship's mercy, always remember and never forget Your lotus feet.

PURPORT

The world in which we live is a miserable place. It is, so to speak, a prison house for the spirit soul. Just as a prisoner cannot move or enjoy life fully, so the living entities who have been conditioned by the laws of material nature cannot experience their actual ever-joyful nature. They cannot have any freedom, because they must suffer four principal miseries—birth, old age, disease, and death. The laws of material nature impose this punishment upon the living entities who have forgotten the Lord and who are busy making plans for lasting happiness in this desert of distress.

By the mercy of the Lord, the pure devotee knows all this very well. Indeed, his whole philosophy of life is based on this understanding. Advancement of knowledge means to understand the naked truth of this world and to not be deluded by the temporary beauty of this phantasmagoria.

The material nature is not at all beautiful, for it is an "imitation peacock." The real peacock is a different thing, and one must have the sense to understand this. Those who are mad after capturing and enjoying the imitation peacock, as well as those who have a pessimistic view of the imitation peacock but lack any positive information of the real peacock—both are illusioned by the modes of material nature. Those who are after the imitation peacock are the fruitive workers, and those who simply condemn the imitation peacock but are ignorant of the real peacock are the empiric philosophers. Disgusted with the mirage of happiness in the material desert, they seek to merge into voidness.

But a pure devotee does not belong to either of these two bewildered classes. Neither aspiring to enjoy the imitation peacock nor condemning it out of disgust, he seeks the real peacock. Thus he is unlike either the deluded fruitive worker or the baffled empiricist. He is above these servants of material nature because he prefers to serve the Lord, the master of material nature. He seeks the substance and does not wish to give it up. The substance is the lotus feet of Mukunda, and King Kulaśekhara, being a most intelligent devotee, prays to gain that substance and not the shadow.

A pure devotee of Lord Nārāyaṇa, or Mukunda, is not at all afraid of any circumstance that may befall him. Despite all difficulties, therefore, such a pure devotee asks nothing from the Lord on his own account. He is not at all afraid if by chance he has to visit the hellish worlds, nor is he eager to enter the kingdom of heaven. For him both these kingdoms are like castles in the air. He is not concerned with either of them, and this is very nicely expressed by King Kulaśekhara in Text 6.

A pure devotee of the Lord like King Kulaśekhara does not pray to God for material wealth, followers, a beautiful wife, or any such imitation peacocks, for he knows the real value of such things. And if by circumstance he is placed in a situation where he possesses such things, he does not try to artificially get out of it by condemnation.

Śrīla Raghunātha dāsa Gosvāmī, a great associate of Lord Caitanya's, was a very rich man's son who had a beautiful wife and all other opulences. When he first met Lord Caitanya at Pāṇihāṭi, a village about forty miles from Calcutta, Raghunātha dāsa asked permission from the Lord to leave his material connections and accompany Him. The Lord refused to accept this proposal and instructed Raghunātha dāsa that it is useless to leave worldly connections out of sentimentality or artificial renunciation. One must have the real thing at heart. If one finds himself entangled in worldly connections, one should behave outwardly like a worldly man but remain inwardly faithful for spiritual realization. That will help one on the progressive march of life. Nobody can cross over the big ocean in a sudden jump. What was possible for Hanumān by the grace of Lord Rāma is not possible for an ordinary man. So to cross the ocean of illusion one should patiently cultivate devotion to the Lord, and in this way one can gradually reach the other side.

Although a pure devotee does not bother himself about what is going to happen next in his material situation, he is always alert not to forget his ultimate aim. King Kulaśekhara therefore prays that he may not forget the lotus feet of the Lord at any time.

To forget one's relationship with the Lord and thus to remain overwhelmed by material hankerings is the most condemned mode of life. This is exactly the nature of animal life. When the living entity is born in a species of lower animals, he completely forgets his relationship with the Lord and therefore remains always busy in the matter of eating, sleeping, fearing, and mating. Modern civilization promotes such a life of forgetfulness, with an improved economic condition for eating and so on. Various agents of the external energy make explicit propaganda to try to root out the very seed of divine consciousness. But this is impossible to do, because although circumstances may choke up a living being's divine consciousness for the time being, it cannot be killed. In his original identity the living entity is indestructible, and so also are his original spiritual qualities. One can kill neither the spirit soul nor his spiritual qualities. To remember the Lord and desire to serve Him are the spiritual qualities of the spirit soul. One can curb down these spiritual qualities by artificial means, but they will be reflected in a perverted way on the mirror of material existence. The spiritual quality of serving the Lord out of transcendental affinity will be pervertedly reflected as love for wine, women, and wealth in different forms. The so-called love of material things—even love for one's country, community, religion, or family, which is accepted as a superior qualification for civilized human beings—is simply a perverted reflection of the love of Godhead dormant in every soul. The position of King Kulaśekhara is therefore the position of a liberated soul, because he does not want to allow his genuine love of God to become degraded into so-called love for material things.

The words *bhave bhave* are very significant here. They mean "birth after birth." Unlike the *jñānīs,* who aspire to merge with the impersonal Absolute and thereby stop the process of repeatedly taking birth, a pure devotee is never afraid of this process. In the *Bhagavad-gītā* (4.9) Lord Kṛṣṇa says that His birth and deeds are all *divyam,* transcendental. In the same chapter (4.5) the Lord says that both He and Arjuna had had many, many previous births, but that while the Lord could remember all of them, Arjuna could not. For the Lord there is no difference between past, present, and future, but for the living being who has forgotten the Lord there is a difference, on account of his being forgetful of the past and ignorant of the future. But a living entity who always remembers the Lord and is thus His constant companion is as transcendentally situated as the Lord Himself. For such a devotee birth and death are one and the same, because he knows that such occurrences are only ephemeral flashes that do not affect his spiritual existence.

We may use a crude example to illustrate the difference between a devotee's death and an ordinary man's death. In her mouth the cat captures both her offspring and her prey, the rat. Such capturings may appear the same, but there is a vast difference between them. While the rat is being carried in the cat's mouth, his sensation is poles apart from that of the cat's offspring. For the rat the capture is a painful death strike, while for the offspring it is a pleasurable caress.

Similarly, the death of an ordinary man is vastly different from a devotee's passing away from the active scene of material existence. The death of an ordinary man occurs against the background of his past good and evil deeds, which determine his next birth. But for a devotee the case is different. Even if the devotee has failed to perfect his devotional service, he is guaranteed to take birth in a good family—a family of learned and devoted *brāhmaṇas* or a family of rich *vaiśyas* (merchants). A person who takes birth in such a family has a good chance to practice devotional service and improve his spiritual condition.

Unfortunately, in this iron age the members of well-to-do families generally misuse their wealth. Instead of improving their spiritual condition, they are misled by faulty association and fall victim to sensuality. To be saved from this faulty association, King Kulaśekhara prays fervently to the Lord that he may never forget His lotus feet in any future birth. A devotee who perfects his devotional service certainly goes back to Godhead without a doubt, so for him there is no question of birth or death. And, as mentioned above, a devotee who does not achieve complete perfection is guaranteed to take his birth in a learned and well-to-do family. But even if a devotee is not given the advantage of good parentage, if he can attain the benediction of always remembering the lotus feet of the Lord, that is greater than any number of material assets. Constant remembrance of the Lord's name, fame, qualities, and so on automatically nullifies the reactions of all vices and invokes the blessings of the Lord. This constant remembrance of the lotus feet of the Lord is possible only when one engages in His active service.

A pure devotee therefore never asks the Lord for wealth, followers, or even a beautiful wife. He simply prays for uninterrupted engagement in the Lord's service. That should be the motto of life for all prospective students in devotional service.

TEXT 4*

नाहं वन्दे तव चरणयोर्द्वन्द्वमद्वन्द्वहेतोः
कुम्भीपाकं गुरुमपि हरे नारकं नापनेतुम् ।
रम्यारामामृदुतनुलता नन्दने नापि रन्तुं
भावे भावे हृदयभवने भावयेयं भवन्तम् ॥४॥

nāhaṁ vande tava caraṇayor dvandvam advandva-hetoḥ
kumbhīpākaṁ gurum api hare nārakaṁ nāpanetum
ramyā-rāmā-mṛdu-tanu-latā nandane nāpi rantuṁ
bhāve bhāve hṛdaya-bhavane bhāvayeyaṁ bhavantam

na—not; *aham*—I; *vande*—pray; *tava*—Your; *caraṇayoḥ*—of the lotus feet; *dvandvam*—to the pair; *advandva*—of release from duality; *hetoḥ*—for the reason; *kumbhīpākam*—the planet of boiling oil; *gurum*—most severe; *api*—either; *hare*—O Hari; *nārakam*—hell; *na*—not; *apanetum*—to avoid; *ramyā*—very beautiful; *rāmā*—of the fair sex; *mṛdu*—soft; *tanu-latā*—of creeperlike bodies; *nandane*—in the pleasure gardens of heaven; *na api*—nor; *rantum*—to enjoy; *bhāve bhāve*—in various rebirths; *hṛdaya*—of my heart; *bhavane*—within the house; *bhāvayeyam*—may I concentrate; *bhavantam*—on You.

TRANSLATION

O Lord Hari, it is not to be saved from the dualities of material existence or the grim tribulations of the Kumbhīpāka hell that I pray to Your lotus feet. Nor is my purpose to enjoy the soft-skinned beautiful women who reside in the gardens of heaven. I pray to Your lotus feet only so that I may remember You alone in the core of my heart, birth after birth.

PURPORT

There are two classes of men: the atheists and the theists. The atheists have no faith in the Supreme Personality of Godhead, while the theists have various degrees of faith in Him.

The atheists are faithless on account of their many misdeeds in their present and past lives. They fall into four categories: (1) the gross materialists, (2) the immoral sinners, (3) the number-one fools, and (4) those who are bewildered by *māyā* despite their mundane erudition. No one among these four classes of atheist ever believes in the Supreme Personality of Godhead, what to speak of offering prayers unto His lotus feet.

The theists, on the other hand, have faith in the Lord and pray to Him with various motives. One attains such a theistic life not by chance but as a result of performing many pious acts in both the present life and the past life. Such pious men also belong to four categories: (1) the needy, (2) those who have fallen into difficulty, (3) those who are inquisitive about the transcendental science, and (4) the genuine philosophers. The philosophers and those who are inquisitive are better than those in categories (1) and (2). But a pure devotee is far above these four classes of pious men, for he is in the transcendental position.

The needy pious man prays to God for a better standard of life, and the pious man who has fallen into material difficulty prays in order to get rid of his trouble. But the inquisitive man and the philosopher do not pray to God for amelioration of mundane problems. They pray for the ability to know Him as He is, and they try to reach Him through science and logic. Such pious men are generally known as theosophists.

Needy pious men pray to God to improve their economic condition because all they know is sense gratification, while those in difficulty ask Him to free them from a hellish life of tribulations. Such ignorant people do not know the value of human life. This life is meant to prepare one to return to the absolute world, the kingdom of God.

A pure devotee is neither a needy man, a man fallen into difficulty, nor an empiric philosopher who tries to approach the Divinity on the strength his own imperfect knowledge. A pure devotee receives knowledge of the Divinity from the right source—the disciplic succession of realized souls who have followed strictly the disciplinary method of devotional service under the guidance of bona fide spiritual masters. It is not possible to know the transcendental nature of the Divinity by dint of one's imperfect sense perception, but the Divinity reveals Himself to a pure devotee in proportion to the transcendental service rendered unto Him.

King Kulaśekhara is a pure devotee, and as such he is not eager to improve himself by the standards of the empiric philosophers, distressed men, or fruitive workers of this world. Pious acts may lead a mundane creature toward the path of spiritual realization, but practical activity in the domain of devotional service to the Lord need not wait for the reactions of pious acts. A pure devotee does not think in terms of his personal gain or loss because he is fully surrendered to the Lord. He is concerned only with the service of the Lord and always engages in that service, and for this reason his heart is the Lord's home. The Lord being absolute, there is no difference between Him and His service. A pure devotee's heart is always filled with ideas about executing the Lord's service, which is bestowed upon the pure devotee through the transparent medium of the spiritual master.

The spiritual master in the authoritative line of disciplic succession is the "son of God," or in other words the Lord's bona fide representative. The proof that he is bona fide is his invincible faith in God, which protects him from the calamity of impersonalism. An impersonalist cannot be a bona fide spiritual master, for such a spiritual master's only purpose in life must be to render service to the Lord. He preaches the message of Godhead as the Lord's appointed agent and has nothing to do with sense gratification or the mundane wrangling of the impersonalists. No one can render devotional service to an impersonal entity because such service implies a reciprocal personal relationship between the servant and the master. In the impersonal school the so-called devotee is supposed to merge with the Lord and lose his separate existence.

Pure devotees like King Kulaśekhara are particularly careful to avoid a process that will end in their becoming one with the existence of the Lord, a state known as *advandva,* nonduality. This is simply spiritual suicide. Out of the five kinds of salvation, *advandva* is the most abominable for a devotee. A pure devotee denounces such oneness with the Lord as worse than going to hell.

As His separated expansions, the living beings are part and parcel of the Lord. The Lord expands Himself into plenary parts and separated parts to enjoy transcendental pastimes, and if a living being refuses to engage in these transcendental blissful pastimes, he is at liberty to merge into the Absolute. This is something like a son's committing suicide instead of living with his father according to the rules the father sets down. By committing suicide, the son thus sacrifices the happiness he could have enjoyed by engaging in a filial loving relationship with his father and enjoying his father's estate. A pure devotee persistently avoids such a criminal policy, and King Kulaśekhara is guiding us to avoid this pitfall.

The king also says that the reason he is praying to the Lord is not to be saved from the Kumbhīpāka hell. Laborers in gigantic iron and steel mills suffer tribulations similar to those in the Kumbhīpāka hell. *Kumbhī* means "pot," and *pāka* means "boiling." So if a person were put into a pot of oil and the pot were set to boiling, he would have some idea of the suffering in Kumbhīpāka hell.

There are innumerable hellish engagements in the modern so-called civilization, and by the grace of the Lord's illusory energy people think these hellish engagements are a great fortune. Modern industrial factories fully equipped with up-to-date machines are so many Kumbhīpāka hells, and the organizers of these enterprises regard them as indispensable for the advancement of economic welfare. The mass of laborers exploited by the organizers directly experience the "welfare" conditions in these factories, but what the organizers do not know is that by the law of *karma* they will in due time become laborers in similar Kumbhīpāka hells.

Intelligent persons certainly want to be saved from such Kumbhīpāka hells, and they pray to God for this benediction. But a pure devotee does not pray in this way. A pure devotee of Nārāyaṇa looks equally upon the happiness enjoyed in heaven, the transcendental bliss of becoming one with the Lord, and the tribulations experienced in the Kumbhīpāka hell. He is not concerned with any of them because he is always engaged in the transcendental loving service of the Lord. By the grace of the Lord, even in the Kumbhīpāka hell a pure devotee can adjust the situation and turn it into Vaikuṇṭha.

The *Bhagavad-gītā* and all other revealed scriptures say that the Lord accompanies every living being in His localized aspect of Paramātmā, the Supersoul. Therefore even a living being destined to reside in the Kumbhīpāka hell is accompanied by his eternal companion, the Lord. But by His inconceivable power the Lord remains aloof from these hellish circumstances, just as the sky remains separate from the air although seemingly mixed with it.

Similarly, the pure devotee of the Lord does not live anywhere in this material world, although He appears to live among mundane creatures. Actually, the devotee lives in Vaikuṇṭha. In this way the Supreme Lord bestows upon His pure devotee the inconceivable power that allows him to stay aloof from all mundane circumstances and reside eternally in the spiritual world. The devotee does not want this power consciously or unconsciously, but the Lord is careful about His devotee, just as a mother is always careful about her little child, who is completely dependent on her care.

A pure devotee like King Kulaśekhara refuses to associate with beautiful soft-skinned women. There are different grades of women on different planets in the universe. Even on the earth there are different types of women who are enjoyed by different types of men. But on higher planets there are women many, many millions of times more beautiful than the women on this planet, and there are also many pleasure abodes where they can be enjoyed. The best of all of these is the Nandana Gardens on Svargaloka. In the Nandana Gardens—a "Garden of Eden"— those who are qualified can enjoy varieties of beautiful women called Apsarās. The demigods generally enjoy the company of the Apsarās in the same way that the great Mogul kings and *nawabs* enjoyed their harems. But these kings and *nawabs* are like straw before the demigods of Svargaloka, which lies in the third stratum of the universe.

The inner tendency to enjoy is in the core of every living being's heart. But in the diseased state of material existence the living being misuses that tendency. The more he increases this diseased, conditioned state, the longer he extends his period of material existence. The *śāstras* advise, therefore, that a living entity should accept only those sense-enjoyable objects necessary for the upkeep of the material body and reject those that are just for sense gratification. In this way he will reduce the tendency for sense enjoyment. This restraint cannot be imposed by force; it must be voluntary.

Such restraint automatically develops in the course of one's executing devotional service. Thus one who is already engaged in devotional service need not restrain his senses artificially. A pure devotee like King Kulaśekhara, therefore, neither desires sense enjoyment nor exerts himself to restrain his senses; rather, he tries only to engage himself in the transcendental loving service of the Lord, without any stop.

TEXT 5*

नास्था धर्मे न वसुनिचये नैव कामोपभोगे
यद्भाव्यं तद्भवतु भगवन्पूर्वकर्मानुरूपम् ।
एतत्प्रार्थ्यं मम बहु मतं जन्मजन्मान्तरेऽपि
त्वत्पादाम्भोरुहयुगगता निश्चला भक्तिरस्तु ॥५॥

nāsthā dharme na vasu-nicaye naiva kāmopabhoge
yad bhāvyaṁ tad bhavatu bhagavan pūrva-karmānurūpam
etat prārthyaṁ mama bahu mataṁ janma-janmāntare 'pi
tvat-pādāmbhoruha-yuga-gatā niścalā bhaktir astu

na—not; *āsthā*—special regard; *dharme*—for religiosity; *na*—nor; *vasu*—of wealth; *nicaye*—for the accumulation; *na eva*—nor even; *kāma-upabhoge*—for sense enjoyment; *yat*— whatever; *bhāvyam*—inevitable; *tat*—that; *bhavatu*—let it happen; *bhagavan*—O Lord; *pūrva*—previous; *karma*—my deeds; *anurūpam*—according to; *etat*—this; *prārthyam*—to be requested; *mama*—by me; *bahu matam*—most desirable; *janma-janma*—birth after birth; *antare*—during; *api*—even; *tvat*—Your; *pāda-amboruha*—of lotus feet; *yuga*—in the pair; *gatā*—resting; *niścalā*—unflinching; *bhaktiḥ*—devotion; *astu*—may there be.

TRANSLATION

O my Lord! I have no attachment for religiosity, or for accumulating wealth, or for enjoying sense gratification. Let these come as they inevitably must, in accordance with my past deeds. But I do pray for this most cherished boon: birth after birth, let me render unflinching devotional service unto Your two lotus feet.

PURPORT

Human beings advance toward God conciousness when they go beyond the gross materialistic life of eating, sleeping, fearing, and mating and begin to develop moral and ethical principles. These principles develop further into religious consciousness, leading to an imaginary conception of God without any practical realization of the truth. These stages of God consciousness are called religiosity, which promises material prosperity of various degrees.

People who develop this conception of religiosity perform sacrifices, give in charity, and undergo different types of austerity and penance, all with a view toward being rewarded with material prosperity. The ultimate goal of such so-called religious people is sense gratification of various kinds. For sense gratification, material prosperity is necessary, and therefore they perform religious rituals with a view toward the resultant material name, fame, and gain.

But genuine religion is different. In Sanskrit such genuine religion is called *dharma,* which means "the essential quality of the living being." The *śāstras* say that this essential quality is to render eternal service, and the proper object of this service is the Supreme Truth, Lord Kṛṣṇa, the Absolute Personality of Godhead. This eternal, transcendental service of the Lord is misdirected under material conditions and takes the shape of (1) the aforementioned religiosity, (2) economic development, (3) sense gratification, and (4) salvation, or the attempt to negate all material variegatedness out of frustration.

Genuine religion, however, does not culminate in either economic development, sense gratification, or salvation. The perfection of religion is to attain complete satisfaction of the spirit soul, and this is accomplished by rendering devotional service to the Lord, who is beyond the perception of the material senses. When the living being directs his eternal service attitude toward the eternal Supreme Being, such service can never be hampered by any sort of material hindrance. Such transcendental service is above even salvation, and therefore it certainly does not aim at any kind of material reward in the shape of name, fame, or gain.

One who engages in the transcendental loving service of the Supreme Being automatically attains detachment from material name, fame, and gain, which are aspired for only by those who do not understand that this name, fame, and gain are merely shadows of the real thing. Material name, fame, and gain are only perverted reflections of the substance—the name, fame, and opulences of the Lord. Therefore the pure devotee of Lord Vāsudeva, enlightened by the transcendental service attitude, has no attraction for such false things as religiosity, economic development, sense gratification, or salvation, the last snare of Māyā.

The purpose of performing real religion is to attain attachment for hearing and chanting the messages of the kingdom of God. Materialistic people are attached to ordinary newspapers on account of their lack of spiritual consciousness. Real religion develops this spiritual consciousness and also attachment for the messages of God, without which all labor in the performance of religious rites is only a waste of energy.

Therefore one should not practice religion with the aim of improving one's economic welfare, nor should one use one's wealth for sense gratification, nor should the frustration of one's plans for sense gratification lead one to aspire for salvation, or liberation from material conditions. Instead of indulging in sense gratification of different grades with the fruits of one's labor, one should work just to maintain the body and soul together, with the aim of inquiring into the ultimate aims and objects of life. In other words, one should inquire into the Absolute Truth.

The Absolute Truth is realized in three phases, namely, the impersonal Brahman, the localized Paramātmā, and the Supreme Personality of Godhead. A person who attains the highest stage of spiritual realization—realization of the Supreme Personality of Godhead—automatically prays as King Kulaśekhara does here.

Only one who renders devotional service to the Lord can attain this stage of indifference to the false and temporary assets of material nature. Such devotional service is not a mental concoction of depraved persons but is an actual process of God realization characterized by full cognizance and detachment and based on the Vedic literature. So-called devotional practices that have no reference to the rules and regulations set down in such books of Vedic literature as the *śruti,* the *smṛti,* the *Purāṇas,* and the *Pañcarātras* are not bona fide. The self-realized souls advise us to reject such pseudodevotional practices, which simply create a disturbance on the path of spiritual realization. Only by sincerely engaging in the service of the Lord according to the injunctions of scripture can one gradually become a qualified devotee of the Lord, and it does not matter whether it takes many repetitions of birth and death, life after life.

TEXT 6*

दिवि वा भुवि वा ममास्तु वासो
नरके वा नरकान्तक प्रकामम् ।

अवधीरितशारदारविन्दौ
चरणौ ते मरणेऽपि चिन्तयामि ॥६॥

divi vā bhuvi vā mamāstu vāso
narake vā narakāntaka prakāmam
avadhīrita-śāradāravindau
caraṇau te maraṇe 'pi cintayāmi

divi—in the abode of the demigods; *vā*—or; *bhuvi*—on the earth, the home of human beings; *vā*—or; *mama*—my; *astu*—may be; *vāsaḥ*—residence; *narake*—in hell; *vā*—or; *naraka-antaka*—O killer of the demon Naraka; *prakāmam*—however You desire; *avadhīrita*—which have defied; *śārada*—of the fall season; *aravindau*—the lotus flowers; *caraṇau*—the two feet; *te*—Your; *maraṇe*—at the time of death; *api*—even; *cintayāmi*—may I remember.

TRANSLATION

O Lord, killer of the demon Naraka! Let me reside either in the realm of the demigods, in the world of human beings, or in hell, as You please. I pray only that at the point of death I may remember Your two lotus feet, whose beauty defies that of the lotus growing in the Śarat season.

PURPORT

As stated before, a pure devotee of the Lord has nothing to do with mundane religiosity, economic development, sense gratification, or salvation, nor is he concerned whether his standard of material existence is the highest or the lowest. To him, heaven and hell are of equal value. He is not afraid of going to hell for the service of the Lord, nor is he glad to live in heaven without the service of the Lord. In any circumstance his consciousness is fixed on the Lord's lotus feet, whose beauty defies the most beautiful lotus flower of the mundane world.

The defiance is due to the transcendental position of the Lord's form, name, qualities, pastimes, and so on. The *śruti mantras* declare that although the Lord has no hands He can accept anything we offer Him with devotion, although He has no feet He can travel anywhere, and although He has no mundane eyes He can see anywhere and everywhere without hindrance. The *Brahma-saṁhitā* describes each of His senses as omnipotent. The mundane eye can see but not hear, but His eyes can see, hear, eat, generate offspring, and so on. The *śruti mantras* say that He impregnates material nature with the seeds of living beings simply by casting His glance at her. He does not need any other kind of intercourse with mother nature to beget the living beings in her womb and become their father.

Therefore any relationship the Lord has with His many devotees—whether fatherhood, sonhood, or any other—is not at all material. The Lord is pure spirit, and only when the living being is in his pure spiritual state can he have all sorts of relationships with Him. Philosophers with a poor fund of knowledge cannot conceive of these positive spiritual relationships between the Lord and the all-spiritual living beings, and thus they simply think in terms of negating material relationships. In this way such philosophers naturally adopt the concept of impersonalism.

By contrast, a pure devotee like King Kulaśekhara has complete knowledge of both matter and spirit. He does not say that everything material is false, yet he has nothing to do with anything material, from heaven down to hell. He fully understands the statement in the *Bhagavad-gītā* that from the lowest planets up to Brahmaloka, the highest planet in the universe, there is no spiritual bliss, which the living beings hanker for. Therefore the pure devotee, being in full knowledge of spiritual life, simultaneously rejects material relationships and cultivates his spiritual relationship with the Lord. In other words, the spiritual knowledge a devotee possesses not only allows him to reject material existence, but it also provides him with an understanding of the reality of positive, eternal spiritual existence. This is the understanding King Kulaśekhara expresses in this prayer.

TEXT 7

चिन्तयामि हरिमेव सन्ततं
मन्दहासमुदिताननाम्बुजम् ।
नन्दगोपतनयं परात् परं
नारदादिमुनिवृन्दवन्दितम् ॥७॥

cintayāmi harim eva santataṁ
manda-hāsa-muditānanāmbujam
nanda-gopa-tanayaṁ parāt paraṁ
nāradādi-muni-vṛnda-vanditam

cintayāmi—I think; *harim*—about Lord Hari; *eva*—indeed; *santatam*—always; *manda*—gentle; *hāsa*—with a smile; *mudita*—joyful; *ānana-ambujam*—whose lotus face; *nanda-gopa*—of the cowherd Nanda; *tanayam*—the son; *parāt param*—the Supreme Absolute Truth; *nārada-ādi*—beginning with Nārada; *muni-vṛnda*—by all the sages; *vanditam*—worshiped.

TRANSLATION

I always think of Lord Hari, whose joyful lotus face bears a gentle smile. Although He is the son of the cowherd Nanda, He is also the Supreme Absolute Truth worshiped by great sages like Nārada.

PURPORT

As King Kulaśekhara thinks of the Lord and remembers His happiness, the king also becomes happy. Lord Kṛṣṇa is eternally happy, but the conditioned soul is mostly unhappy. When we live in forgetfulness of our spiritual nature, even our so-called bliss is illusion—it is unsatisfying, flickering pleasure (*capala-sukha*). The poet Govinda dāsa expresses this in his song *Bhajhuṁ re mana:* "What assurance is there in all one's wealth, youthfulness, sons, and family members? This life is tilting like a drop of water on a lotus petal. Therefore you should always serve the divine feet of Lord Hari."

Another Vaiṣṇava poet, Narottama dāsa Ṭhākura, has expressed the happiness of the Supreme in a song addressed to Lord Caitanya and Lord Nityānanda: *hā hā prabhu nityānanda premānanda-sukhī kṛpā-balo-kana koro āmi baḍo duḥkhī:* "My dear Lord Nityānanda, You are always joyful in spiritual bliss. Since You always appear very happy, I have come to You because I am most unhappy. If You kindly cast Your glance upon me, I may also become happy."

In this prayer King Kulaśekhara reveals himself to be at the stage of spontaneous love of God, in which the devotee goes beyond mere formal ceremonies and ritual recitations and thinks of Lord Hari always. This is the actual standard of happiness in devotional service. Such constant remembrance of the Lord is possible through constant chanting of His name. As Lord Caitanya recommends in His *Śikṣāṣṭaka* (3), *kīrtanīyaḥ sadā hariḥ:* "One should always chant the holy name of the Lord." In this way one will always be happy in the joy of Lord Kṛṣṇa. The Lord's happiness is always increasing, like an ever-expanding ocean (*ānandāmbudhi-vardhanam*), and the living entity is meant to dive into that ocean because his original nature is to be ever-blissful in contact with the Lord.

King Kulaśekhara further hints at the unlimited happiness of Kṛṣṇa consciousness when he describes Lord Kṛṣṇa as the son of Nanda Gopa. Kṛṣṇa is the Lord of Vaikuṇṭha, and He expands Himself as the *catur-vyūha,* as the *puruṣa-avatāras,* and as many other forms. But His original form is a cowherd boy in Goloka Vṛndāvana. He came to Vṛndāvana-dhāma within this world to reciprocate loving exchanges with His pure devotees here who wished to be His friends, parents, and lovers. They cherished the desire to serve the Lord in intimate ways, and they finally fulfilled it after, as Śrīla Prabhupāda says in his *Kṛṣṇa* book, "accumulating heaps of pious activities." In other words, after they had perfected their loving devotion to the Lord through many lives of service, He appeared in person to reciprocate with them in their specific mood.

Kṛṣṇa enjoyed playing as the son of Nanda. For example, Kṛṣṇa would sometimes delight His parents by carrying His father's wooden slippers on His head, just like an ordinary child. And Kṛṣṇa would also enjoy His magnificent pastimes in Dvārakā, where He lived in unequaled opulence in 16,108 palaces with an equal number of queens. Nārada once visited the Lord at Dvārakā and saw Him engaging in varioius pastimes in His many palaces. At that time Nārada became astounded and described Him as the source of all opulences.

There is no contradiction between Kṛṣṇa's charmingly sweet pastimes in the simple village of Vṛndāvana and His magnificently opulent pastimes in Dvārakā. All of the Lords pastimes are oceans of happiness. And the devotee who can always think of the Lord performing any of His multifarious pastimes dives into that ocean. Even in this world, one who always thinks of the Lord will forget all material miseries and enter the spiritual abode.

TEXT 8

करचरणसरोजे कान्तिमन्नेत्रमीने
श्रममुषि भुजवीचिव्याकुलेऽगाधमार्गे ।
हरिसरसि विगाह्यापीय तेजोजलौघं
भवमरुपरिखिन्नः क्लेशमद्य त्यजामि ॥८॥

kara-caraṇa-saroje kāntiman-netra-mīne
śrama-muṣi bhuja-vīci-vyākule 'gādha-mārge
hari-sarasi vigāhyāpīya tejo-jalaugham
bhava-maru-parikhinnaḥ kleśam adya tyajāmi

kara—hands; *caraṇa*—and feet; *saroje*—whose lotuses; *kānti-mat*—shining; *netra*—eyes; *mīne*—whose fish; *śrama*—exhaustion; *muṣi*—robbing; *bhuja*—of arms; *vīci*—by waves; *vyākule*—agitated; *agādha*—fathomless; *mārge*—whose movement; *hari*—of Lord Hari; *sarasi*—in the lake; *vigāhya*—by diving; *āpīya*—drinking fully; *tejaḥ*—of His splendor; *jala*—of water; *ogham*—the flood; *bhava*—of material existence; *maru*—in the desert; *parikhinnaḥ*—worn out; *kleśam*—distress; *adya*—today; *tyajāmi*—I will abandon.

TRANSLATION

The desert of material existence has exhausted me. But today I will cast aside all troubles by diving into the lake of Lord Hari and drinking freely of the abundant waters of His splendor. The lotuses in that lake are His hands and feet, and the fish are His brilliant shining eyes. That lake's water relieves all fatigue and is agitated by the waves His arms create. Its current flows deep beyond fathoming.

PURPORT

In this prayer King Kulaśekhara employs an elaborate metaphor comparing the Lord's all-attractive form to a rejuvenating lake. If a devotee dives into that lake and drinks its waters, all his exhaustion from material life will go away. We simply have to plunge into devotional service by hearing about Kṛṣṇa, chanting His glories, and remembering Him. Why don't we all do it? It is illusion that makes us think there is no relief here, or that the lake is a mirage. Or, out of foolish attachment to material activities, we may think it's irresponsible to dive into the ocean of pleasure that is Kṛṣṇa consciousness. "Where is that lake?" we think. "I would gladly jump into it if I could find it. But it sounds like the legendary fountain of youth."

When we show the nondevotees the Lord's form and invite them to serve Him, they refuse. They think He's just an ordinary man or a mythical figure. But there *is* a "lake of Lord Hari," and there are aquatics sporting in it—the Lord's pure devotees, who have no cares or fear or anger or lust. They have dived into that lake and are free of all material exhaustion. In body, mind, and spirit we grow tired, but the waters of this lake relieve all our fatigue.

Elsewhere in the Vedic literature we hear of lakes such as Bindu-sarovara, where Devahūti was revived and made beautiful again after her long austerities. But the effect of immersing oneself in the lake of Lord Hari is not the restoration of youth, which will soon be exhausted again. It is eternal relief from *saṁsāra,* the repetition of birth and death.

We may attain attraction to the Lord's form by worshiping the Deity in the temple and hearing descriptions of His form in the *śāstra.* Also, chanting and hearing His names evokes attraction to His form, which the Lord eventually manifests to the pure chanter. As we become attracted to the form of the Lord, we will give up trying to enjoy other forms, an effort that simply leads to exhaustion. We will know then that only Kṛṣṇa can satisfy us.

TEXT 9

सरसिजनयने सशङ्खचक्रे
मुरभिदि मा विरमस्व चित्त रन्तुम् ।
सुखतरमपरं न जातु जाने
हरिचरणस्मरणामृतेन तुल्यम् ॥९॥

sarasija-nayane sa-śaṅkha-cakre
mura-bhidi mā viramasva citta rantum
sukha-taram aparaṁ na jātu jāne
hari-caraṇa-smaraṇāmṛtena tulyam

sarasi-ja—like the lotus flower born in a lake; *nayane*—whose eyes; *sa*—together with; *śaṅkha*—His conch; *cakre*—and disc weapon; *mura-bhidi*—in the annihilator of the demon Mura; *mā viramasva*—please never cease; *citta*—O mind; *rantum*—to enjoy; *sukha-taram*—extremely pleasurable; *aparam*—anything else; *na*—not; *jātu*—at all; *jāne*—I know; *hari-caraṇa*—of the feet of Lord Hari; *smaraṇa*—of the remembrance; *amṛtena*—the immortal nectar; *tulyam*—equal to.

TRANSLATION

O mind, please never stop taking pleasure in thinking of the Mura demon's destroyer, who has lotus eyes and bears the conch and disc weapon. Indeed, I know of nothing else that gives such extreme pleasure as meditating on Lord Hari's divine feet.

PURPORT

From his own experience, King Kulaśekhara is speaking of how delightful it is to think of Kṛṣṇa. That thinking is his greatest pleasure in life. As a king he had access to many worldly pleasures, but they all counted as nothing compared to meditation on the Lord's lotus feet. This Kṛṣṇa meditation is available for all, and the Supreme Lord and His representatives want everyone to enjoy it. Thus Lord Kṛṣṇa says in the *Bhagavad-gītā*, "Always think of Me." This meditation is not only for philosophers and poets. Though Arjuna was a military man, Lord Kṛṣṇa instructed him, "Remember Me and fight."

The Vedic literature, prepared by Śrīla Vyāsadeva and filled with narrations of the Lord and His devotees, is meant to help us remember the Lord always. These books teach us how to divert our mind from ordinary thoughts, which are filled with business, entertainment, speculation, and the like, and fix it on the Supreme Lord in His personal feature. Otherwise, numerous worldly thoughts will absorb us: News of politics, for instance, is always bombarding us via TV, radio, and the print media. Also, our personal economic affairs are themselves fully absorbing. And to put up with anxieties, we can take part in diversions like videos, music, intoxication, and sex stimulation. Wasting time with mundane thoughts is nothing new, but today the pace, variety, and intensity of diversions grabbing for our attention seem to have increased.

Thus although meditation on God is as essential as ever, one may conclude that it is impossible nowadays. However, by the grace of Śrīla Prabhupāda and the Kṛṣṇa consciousness movement he founded, we can absorb the mind in thoughts of the Lord even in this age. If one lives in a city with an ISKCON temple, one can directly visit the Deity of Lord Viṣṇu, as King Kulaśekhara did. Even on the way to work one may find time to stop and briefly see the Lord in the temple. If one lives far from a temple, one can still read Śrīla Prabhupāda's books, correspond with devotees, listen to devotional recordings, subscribe to regular Kṛṣṇa conscious publications, and, of course, chant the Hare Kṛṣṇa *mantra* alone or with friends. Thus in these and many other ways, meditation on Kṛṣṇa is available to those who want it.

Here King Kulaśekhara specifically mentions meditation upon the feet of the Lord. Such meditation implies humility and indicates that the meditator desires shelter under the Lord's protection. Indeed, the Lord's lotus feet symbolize that shelter. Elsewhere the Vedic literature describes the Lord's lotus feet as umbrellas shielding the devotees from material life. So a devotee is satisfied meditating on the Lord's feet, although he sometimes meditates on other parts of the Lord's body. We should remember, however, that although the lotus feet of the Lord symbolize the total shelter He extends toward His devotees, there is nothing "symbolic" about them: they are always to be thought of in a personal, literal sense.

Once some *haṭha-yoga* students asked Śrīla Prabhupāda if there was a śāstric reference specifically stating that transcendentalists who regard the Absolute Truth as impersonal would fall down. Prabhupāda quoted the following verse from *Śrīmad-Bhāgavatam* (10.2.32):

ye 'nye 'ravindākṣa vimukta-māninas
tvayy asta-bhāvād aviśuddha-buddhayaḥ
āruhya kṛcchreṇa paraṁ padaṁ tataḥ
patanty adho 'nādṛta yuṣmad-aṅghrayaḥ

"O lotus-eyed Lord, although nondevotees who accept severe austerities and penances to achieve the highest position may think themselves liberated, their intelligence is impure. They fall down from their position of imagined superiority because they have no regard for Your lotus feet." After quoting the verse, Prabhupāda said, "'Feet' means 'person.'"

In conclusion, then, we should have firm faith that the Absolute Truth is the Supreme Person, Kṛṣṇa, that His body is all-blissful, and that His feet are worth meditating upon.

TEXT 10

माभीर्मन्दमनो विचिन्त्य बहुधा यामीश्चिरं यातना
नैवामी प्रभवन्ति पापरिपवः स्वामी ननु श्रीधरः ।
आलस्यं व्यपनीय भक्तिसुलभं ध्यायस्व नारायणं
लोकस्य व्यसनापनोदनकरो दासस्य किं न क्षमः ॥१०॥

mābhīr manda-mano vicintya bahudhā yāmīś ciraṁ yātanā
naivāmī prabhavanti pāpa-ripavaḥ svāmī nanu śrīdharaḥ
ālasyaṁ vyapanīya bhakti-sulabhaṁ dhyāyasva nārāyaṇaṁ
lokasya vyasanāpanodana-karo dāsasya kiṁ na kṣamaḥ

mā bhīḥ—do not be afraid; *manda*—foolish; *manaḥ*—O mind; *vicintya*—thinking; *bahudhā*—repeatedly; *yāmīḥ*—caused by Yamarāja, the lord of death; *ciram*—long-lasting; *yātanāḥ*—about the torments; *na*—not; *eva*—indeed; *amī*—these; *prabhavanti*—are effective; *pāpa*—sinful reactions; *ripavaḥ*—the enemies; *svāmī*—master; *nanu*—is He not; *śrī-dharaḥ*—the maintainer of the goddess of fortune; *ālasyam*—sloth; *vyapanīya*—driving off; *bhakti*—by devotional service; *su-labham*—who is easily attained; *dhyāyasva*—just meditate; *nārāyaṇam*—upon the Supreme Lord Nārāyaṇa; *lokasya*—of the world; *vyasana*—the troubles; *apanodana-karaḥ*—who dispels; *dāsasya*—for His servant; *kim*—what; *na*—not; *kṣamaḥ*—capable.

TRANSLATION

O foolish mind, stop your fearful fretting about the extensive torments imposed by Yamarāja. How can your enemies, the sinful reactions you have accrued, even touch you? After all, is your master not the Supreme Lord, the husband of Goddess Śrī? Cast aside all hesitation and concentrate your thoughts on Lord Nārāyaṇa, whom one very easily attains through devotional service. What can that dispeller of the whole world's troubles not do for His own servant?

PURPORT

In a very positive mood, King Kulaśekhara reminds us that as long as we are under the protection of the supreme, all-powerful Lord, no harm can come to us, even that which our own sinful reactions would normally bring us. Lord Kṛṣṇa also orders Arjuna in the *Bhagavad-gītā* (9.31), "Declare it boldly: My devotee will never be vanquished."

Sinful life and its reactions are certainly serious matters, not to be easily dismissed. Yamarāja metes out hellish torments to all sinful living beings. But the process of *bhakti* is so potent that it drives away all sinful reactions as if they were merely enemies one might see in a bad dream. In Text 15 King Kulaśekhara will recommend the chanting of the holy name of Kṛṣṇa as the best way to attain freedom from the miseries of birth and death. Nāmācārya Haridāsa Ṭhākura concurs, declaring that even the shadow of pure chanting of the holy names, known as *nāmābhāsa,* destroys the entire stock of sins one has accumulated for many lifetimes and thus grants liberation.

The devotees' claim to victory over birth and death is not an idle boast, but it requires full surrender to Lord Hari. The Lord offers this benediction to the unalloyed servant of His servant, and not to others. As long as one tries to protect oneself with wealth and worldly power, one will be an easy victim for powerful Māyā. The *jīva* who is serious about freeing himself from *saṁsāra* does not, therefore, pretend to act on his or her own prowess but always follows the authorized directions of the Supreme Lord and His representatives. Only such a dependent servitor of the Lord, under His full protection, can be confident of conquering birth and death.

In this prayer King Kulaśekhara mentions Yamarāja, the lord of death, as the cause of long-lasting torments. But such suffering is not for the Lord's devotees. Yamarāja himself once instructed his servants, the Yamadūtas, that those who chant the holy names of the Lord were not under Yama's jurisdiction. Yamarāja said, "Generally [the devotees] never commit sinful activities, but even if by mistake or because of bewilderment or illusion they sometimes commit sinful acts, they are protected from sinful reactions because they always chant the Hare Kṛṣṇa *mantra*" (*Bhāg.* 6.3.26). Yamarāja told his followers they should not even go near the devotees. The Vaiṣṇavas are always protected by Lord Viṣṇu's club, and thus neither Lord Brahmā nor even the time factor can chastise them.

Śrīla Prabhupāda said that when a devotee receives initiation from his spiritual master he is freed from his karmic reactions. Pains and pleasures that may appear like continuing karmic reactions are merely the residual effects of nondevotional activities, like the last revolutions of an electric fan after it's been unplugged. But everything depends on the sincere execution of devotional service. One who again regularly transgresses the laws of God, even after taking the vows of initiation, is once more subject to the merciless dealings of the material nature.

TEXT 11

भवजलधिगतानां द्वन्द्ववाताहतानां
सुतदुहितृकलत्रत्राणभारार्दितानाम् ।
विषमविषयतोये मज्जतामप्लवानां
भवति शरणमेको विष्णुपोतो नराणाम् ॥११॥

bhava-jaladhi-gatānāṁ dvandva-vātāhatānāṁ
suta-duhitṛ-kalatra-trāṇa-bhārārditānām
viṣama-viṣaya-toye majjatām aplavānāṁ
bhavati śaraṇam eko viṣṇu-poto narāṇām

bhava—of material existence; *jaladhi*—in the ocean; *gatānām*—who are present; *dvandva*—of material dualities; *vāta*—by the wind; *āhatānām*—struck; *suta*—sons; *duhitṛ*—daughters; *kalatra*—and wives; *trāṇa*—of protecting; *bhāra*—by the burden; *arditānām*—distressed; *viṣama*—perilous; *viṣaya*—of sense gratification; *toye*—in the water; *majjatām*—drowning; *aplavānām*—having no vessel to carry them away; *bhavati*—is; *śaraṇam*—the shelter; *ekaḥ*—only; *viṣṇu-potaḥ*—the boat that is Lord Viṣṇu; *narāṇām*—for people in general.

TRANSLATION

The people in this vast ocean of birth and death are being blown about by the winds of material dualities. As they flounder in the perilous waters of sense indulgence, with no boat to help them, they are sorely distressed by the need to protect their sons, daughters, and wives. Only the boat that is Lord Viṣṇu can save them.

PURPORT

Materialists sometimes philosophize that dualities such as heat and cold provide an interesting variety or spice to life. In truth, however, although we may romanticize about life in this temporary world of duality, its main quality is misery. Prahlāda Mahārāja has described this world as a place where we meet up with things we don't want and are separated from what we love. We either hanker for what we lack, or we lament upon losing something valuable. Whenever we seem to run into smooth sailing on the sea of human affairs, we know, either consciously or at the back of our minds, that we are being pursued by Time, the ultimate destroyer.

Attempting to expand our happiness, we select a marriage partner and raise a family. We may sometimes see our family members as protectors against the ravages of fate, but they prove to be, in Śrīla Prabhupāda's immortal words, "fallible soldiers." Our search for security and happiness through family life merely increases our jeopardy and pain. As Nārada Muni said when King Citraketu's infant son died: "My dear king, now you are actually experiencing the misery of a person who has sons and daughters. O king, . . . a person's wife, his house, the opulence of his kingdom, and his various other opulences and objects of sense perception are all the same in that they are temporary. One's kingdom, military power, treasury, servants, ministers, friends, and relatives are all causes of fear, illusion, lamentation, and distress. They are like a *gandharva-nagara,* a nonexistent palace that one imagines to exist in the forest. Because they are impermanent, they are no better than illusions, dreams, and mental concoctions" (*Bhāg.* 6.15.23).

When distress strikes it is natural to seek shelter, and at such times a pious soul turns to the Supreme Lord, our only protector. When Gajendra, the king of the elephants, was attacked in the water by a crocodile, he soon realized that none of his wives or fellow elephants could save him. "They cannot do anything," said Gajendra. "It is by the will of providence that I have been attacked by this crocodile, and therefore I shall seek the shelter of the Supreme Personality of Godhead, who is always the shelter of everyone, even of great personalities" (*Bhāg.* 8.2.32).

None of us wants calamities, yet when they come they may serve as an impetus to surrender to Lord Kṛṣṇa. Thus Queen Kuntī prayed,

vipadaḥ santu tāḥ śaśvat tatra tatra jagad-guro
bhavato darśanaṁ yat syād apunar bhava-darśanam

"I wish that all those calamities would happen again and again so that we could see You again and again, for seeing You means that we will no longer see repeated births and deaths" (*Bhāg.* 1.8.25).

TEXT 12

भवजलधिमगाधं दुस्तरं निस्तरेयं
कथमहमिति चेतो मा स्म गाः कातरत्वम् ।
सरसिजदृशि देवे तारकी भक्तिरेका
नरकभिदि निषण्णा तारयिष्यत्यवश्यम् ॥१२॥

bhava-jaladhim agādhaṁ dustaraṁ nistareyaṁ
katham aham iti ceto mā sma gāḥ kātaratvam
sarasija-dṛśi deve tārakī bhaktir ekā
naraka-bhidi niṣaṇṇā tārayiṣyaty avaśyam

bhava—of material existence; *jaladhim*—the ocean; *agādham*—fathomless; *dustaram*—impossible to cross; *nistareyam*—will cross beyond; *katham*—how; *aham*—I; *iti*—thus; *cetaḥ*—my dear mind; *mā sma gāḥ*—please do not come; *kātaratvam*—to complete distress; *sarasi-ja*—like a lotus; *dṛśi*—whose eyes; *deve*—unto the Lord; *tārakī*—deliver; *bhaktiḥ*—the personality of Devotion; *ekā*—only; *naraka*—of the demon Naraka; *bhidi*—in the destroyer; *niṣaṇṇā*—reposed; *tārayiṣyati*—will bring you across; *avaśyam*—inevitably.

TRANSLATION

Dear mind, do not bewilder yourself by anxiously thinking, How can I cross this fathomless and impassable ocean of material existence? There is one who can save you—Devotion. If you offer her to the lotus-eyed Lord, the killer of Narakāsura, she will carry you across this ocean without fail.

PURPORT

The devotee is not afraid of the miseries of material existence. He is confident that Kṛṣṇa will save him. Although the forces of destruction are more powerful that any mortal, the devotee is like a tiny bird protected by its parents. The Supreme Lord assures us, "Declare it boldly, O Arjuna, that my devotee never perishes" (Bg. 9.31).

However, if one seeks the protection of the Lord through some means other than devotion, one will fail. Kṛṣṇa is not impressed by anything but devotion. For example, in the *Bhagavad-gītā* (9.26) He encourages the devotee to offer Him food in order to increase the devotee's loving relationship with Him: "If one offers Me with love and devotion a leaf, a flower, a fruit, or water, I will accept it." The Supreme Lord does not want any food or flowers in and of themselves, but when His devotee offers them with *bhakti,* He is very attracted and inclined to reciprocate His devotee's love.

Unless the Supreme Lord is pleased with our service, He will not reveal Himself (*nāhaṁ prakāśaḥ sarvasya yogamāyā-samāvṛtaḥ*). And without His personal intervention, a soul will remain stranded in the cycle of birth and death, despite all material qualifications. In his prayers to Lord Nṛsiṁha, Prahlāda Mahārāja confirms that *bhakti* alone can satisfy the Lord: "One may possess wealth, an aristocratic family, beauty, austerity, education, sensory expertise, luster, influence, physical strength, diligence, intelligence, and mystic yogic power, but I think that even by all these qualifications one cannot satisfy the Supreme Personality of Godhead. However, one can satisfy the Lord simply by devotional service. Gajendra did this, and thus the Lord was satisfied with him" (*Bhāg.* 7.9.9).

Even though one is serving a spiritual master, one may doubt the efficacy of *bhakti.* But King Kulaśekhara assures his mind that there is no need for anxiety. If we contemplate the abysmal depth and impassable breadth of the material ocean, or if we frighten ourselves by dwelling on the torments of hell, then we will become paralyzed and unable to carry out normal activities. There is no need for such fear if one is situated sincerely in devotional service. As the *brāhmaṇa* from Avantīdeśa said,

etāṁ sa āsthāya parātma-niṣṭhām
adhyāsitāṁ pūrvatamair maharṣibhiḥ

ahaṁ tariṣyāmi duranta-pāraṁ
tamo mukundāṅghri-niṣevayaiva

"I shall cross over the insurmountable ocean of nescience by being firmly fixed in the service of the lotus feet of Kṛṣṇa. This was approved by the previous *ācāryas,* who were fixed in firm devotion to the Lord, Paramātmā, the Supreme Personality of Godhead" (*Bhāg.* 11.23.57).

TEXT 13

तृष्णातोये मदनपवनोद्धूतमोहोर्मिमाले
दारावर्ते तनयसहजग्राहसङ्घाकुले च ।
संसाराख्ये महति जलधौ मज्जतां नस्त्रिधामन्
पादाम्भोजे वरद भवतो भक्तिनावं प्रयच्छ ॥१३॥

tṛṣṇā-toye madana-pavanoddhūta-mohormi-māle
dārāvarte tanaya-sahaja-grāha-saṅghākule ca
saṁsārākhye mahati jaladhau majjatāṁ nas tri-dhāman
pādāmbhoje vara-da bhavato bhakti-nāvaṁ prayaccha

tṛṣṇā—thirst; *toye*—whose water; *madana*—of Cupid; *pavana*—by the winds; *uddhūta*—stirred up; *moha*—illusion; *ūrmi*—of waves; *māle*—rows; *dāra*—wife; *āvarte*—whose whirlpool; *tanaya*—sons; *sahaja*—and brothers; *grāha*—of sharks; *saṅgha*—with hordes; *ākule*—crowded; *ca*—and; *saṁsāra-ākhye*—called *saṁsāra; mahati*—vast; *jaladhau*—in the ocean; *majjatām*—who are drowning; *naḥ*—to us; *tri-dhāman*—O Lord of the three worlds; *pāda*—to the feet; *ambhoje*—lotuslike; *vara-da*—O giver of benedictions; *bhavataḥ*—of Your good self; *bhakti*—of devotion; *nāvam*—the boat; *prayaccha*—please bestow.

TRANSLATION

O Lord of the three worlds, we are drowning in the vast ocean of *saṁsāra,* which is filled with the waters of material hankering, with many waves of illusion whipped up by the winds of lust, with whirlpools of wives, and with vast schools of sharks and other sea monsters who are our sons and brothers. O giver of all benedictions, please grant me a place on the boat of devotion that is Your lotus feet.

PURPORT

In this nightmare vision, all the dear and familiar things in life become fearful. And yet this is an accurate assessment of material reality. King Kulaśekhara's oceanic metaphors are not fanciful, but show us vividly what actually *is.*

There is a common saying that a drowning person suddenly sees his whole life pass before him. But we never hear what happens to the person after death. The atheist assumes that when we die it is all over and we rest in peace. But according to Vedic knowledge, there is life after death. "One who has taken birth is sure to die, and after death one is sure to take birth again" (Bg. 2.27). If the conditioned soul sees his life pass before him at death, it is usually with regret. His strong attachment to life-long companions and family members becomes a big weight that drags him down into repeated birth and death.

Therefore it is better for a person to see the fearfulness inherent in material life before it is too late to rectify his consciousness. When he begins to realize that there is great danger in the way he is leading his life, enjoying a false sense of security within his orbit of friends and relatives, then he must by all means try to change the situation by taking up devotional service to the Lord. If he is fortunate he can convince his friends and relatives to also change and lead a life dedicated to God consciousness. But if he cannot change them, then he should at least save himself. As Prahlāda Mahārāja told his demoniac father, Hiraṇyakaśipu:

tat sādhu manye 'sura-varya dehināṁ
sadā samudvigna-dhiyām asad-grahāt
hitvātma-pātaṁ gṛham andha-kūpaṁ
vanaṁ gato yad dharim āśrayeta

"O best of the *asuras,* king of the demons, as far as I have learned from my spiritual master, any person who has accepted a temporary body and temporary household life is certainly embarrassed by anxiety because of having fallen into a dark well where there is no water but only suffering. One should give up this position and go to the forest. More clearly, one should go to Vṛndāvana, where only Kṛṣṇa consciousness is prevalent, and should thus take shelter of the Supreme Personality of Godhead" (*Bhāg.* 7.5.5).

It is not an easy thing to wake up from the complacency of ordinary life. Everyone knows that life is full of difficulties, but we tend to think that our family members and friends are our only solace. But as Kulaśekhara and other Vedic sages point out, in materialistic life our family members are like vicious beasts attacking us. To convey this unpalatable truth, Jaḍa Bharata related to King Rahūgaṇa an allegory about the forest of material enjoyment. In this context he said, "My dear king, family members in this material world go under the names of wives and children, but actually they behave like tigers and jackals."

Several times in the *Mukunda-mālā-stotra,* the poet compares the material world to the sea, and the Lord (or His lotus feet) to a boat that can rescue us. The metaphor is excellent, for no matter how expert a swimmer a person may be, he cannot survive on his own in the rough and vast expanses of the ocean. So our attempt to swim the ocean of material life on our own strength, encouraged by our family and friends, is as futile as the attempt of the lone swimmer at sea. We should turn to our only rescuer, the Lord, and with utmost sincerity thank Him for coming to save us.

TEXT 14

पृथ्वी रेणुरणुः पयांसि कणिकाः फल्गुः स्फुलिङ्गो लघुस्
तेजो निःश्वसनं मरुत्तनुतरं रन्ध्रं सुसूक्ष्मं नभः ।
क्षुद्रा रुद्रपितामहप्रभृतयः कीटाः समस्ताः सुरा
दृष्टे यत्र स तारको विजयते श्रीपादधूलीकणः ॥१४॥

pṛthvī reṇur aṇuḥ payāṁsi kaṇikāḥ phalguḥ sphuliṅgo laghus
tejo niḥśvasanaṁ marut tanu-taraṁ randhraṁ su-sūkṣmaṁ nabhaḥ
kṣudrā rudra-pitāmaha-prabhṛtayaḥ kīṭāḥ samastāḥ surā
dṛṣṭe yatra sa tārako vijayate śrī-pāda-dhūlī-kaṇaḥ

pṛthvī—the earth; *reṇuḥ*—a piece of dust; *aṇuḥ*—atomic; *payāṁsi*—the waters (of the oceans); *kaṇikāḥ*—drops; *phalguḥ*—tiny; *sphuliṅgaḥ*—a spark; *laghuḥ*—insignificant; *tejaḥ*—the totality of elemental fire; *niḥ-śvasanam*—a sigh; *marut*—the wind; *tanu-taram*—very faint; *randhram*—a hole; *su*—very; *sūkṣmam*—small; *nabhaḥ*—the ethereal sky; *kṣūdrāḥ*—petty; *rudra*—Lord Śiva; *pitāmaha*—Lord Brahmā; *prabhṛtayaḥ*—and the like; *kīṭāḥ*—insects; *samastāḥ*—all; *surāḥ*—the demigods; *dṛṣṭe*—having been seen; *yatra*—where; *saḥ*—He; *tārakaḥ*—the deliverer; *vijayate*—is victorious; *śrī*—divine; *pāda*—from the feet; *dhūlī*—of dust; *kaṇaḥ*—a particle.

TRANSLATION

Once our savior has been seen, the whole earth becomes no greater than a speck of dust, all the waters of the ocean become mere droplets, the totality of fire becomes a minute spark, the winds become just a faint sigh, and the expanse of space becomes a tiny hole. Great lords like Rudra and Grandfather Brahmā become insignificant, and all the demigods become like small insects. Indeed, even one particle of dust from our Lord's feet conquers all.

PURPORT

Lord Kṛṣṇa is unlimited: no one is greater than or equal to Him. Therefore it is impossible to compare Him with anyone else, even if we wish to make a favorable comparison. He is unique. Everything depends on Him, and He is the only provider (*eko bahūnāṁ yo vidadhāti kāmān*). Therefore to say that God is greater than all others is insufficient praise.

But to bring the reality of the Godhead more vividly to focus in our limited minds (which are always prone to making comparisons), King Kulaśekhara here gives us metaphors that stress the supreme greatness of the Lord. He compares the Supreme Lord to persons and things we might think are the very greatest. Those who reject the personal conception of God, such as pantheists, think that the earth itself is God. Some impersonalists think that the sky is the greatest manifestation, and so they consider it to be God. Demigod-worshipers consider Rudra or Brahmā the supreme person, or they think all gods are equal. Thus Kulaśekhara's metaphors serve to dismantle all these misconceptions.

This verse expresses King Kulaśekhara's mood of awe and reverence as he contemplates the Supreme Lord's magnificent power and opulence. Many pure *bhaktas* go beyond this appreciation of the Lord in His opulent majesty and come to enjoy intimate loving exchanges with Him. But regardless of one's ultimate relationship with the Lord, when one starts one's devotional career, one must be trained to appreciate the greatness of the Supreme Lord. Therefore in the *Bhagavad-gītā* (9.8) Kṛṣṇa teaches His friend Arjuna, "The whole cosmic order is under Me. Under My will it is automatically manifested again and again, and under My will it is annihilated at the end."

Because the Supreme Lord's potencies are unlimited, they are also inconceivable. For example, Kṛṣṇa creates all the species of life and yet He has no connection with them. The *jīva* souls have no awareness of how the cosmic process is taking place, yet by the will of the Lord they are sometimes supplied bodies, allowed to maintain themselves for awhile, and then, without their knowledge or control, they are annihilated. But He whose will directs all these changes is not involved with it.

Glorifying the Lord as King Kulaśekhara does in this prayer awakens in us the proper mood of appreciation for the Lord's greatness and also helps us understand our position as His insignificant servants.

TEXT 15

हे लोकाः शृणुत प्रसूतिमरणव्याधेश्चिकित्सामिमां
योगज्ञाः समुदाहरन्ति मुनयो यां याज्ञवल्क्यादयः ।
अन्तर्ज्योतिरमेयमेकममृतं कृष्णाख्यमापीयतां
तत्पीतं परमौषधं वितनुते निर्वाणमात्यन्तिकम् ॥१५॥

he lokāḥ śṛṇuta prasūti-maraṇa-vyādheś cikitsām imāṁ
yoga-jñāḥ samudāharanti munayo yāṁ yājñavalkyādayaḥ
antar-jyotir ameyam ekam amṛtaṁ kṛṣṇākhyam āpīyatāṁ
tat pītaṁ paramauṣadhaṁ vitanute nirvāṇam ātyantikam

he lokāḥ—O people of the world; *śṛṇuta*—just hear; *prasūti*—of birth; *maraṇa*—and death; *vyādheḥ*—for the disease; *cikitsām*—about the treatment; *imām*—this; *yoga-jñāḥ*—experts in knowledge of mystic *yoga; samudāharanti*—recommend; *munayaḥ*—sagacious; *yām*—which; *yājñavalkya-ādayaḥ*—such as Yājñavalkya; *antaḥ*—inner; *jyotiḥ*—light; *ameyam*—immeasurable; *ekam*—only; *amṛtam*—immortal; *kṛṣṇa-ākhyam*—the name of Kṛṣṇa; *āpīyatām*—just drink; *tat*—it; *pītam*—being drunk; *parama*—supreme; *auṣadham*—medicine; *vitanute*—bestows; *nirvāṇam*—liberation; *ātyantikam*—absolute.

TRANSLATION

O people, please hear of this treatment for the disease of birth and death! It is the name of Kṛṣṇa. Recommended by Yājñavalkya and other expert *yogīs* steeped in wisdom, this boundless, eternal inner light is the best medicine, for when drunk it bestows complete and final liberation. Just drink it!

PURPORT

Devotees are always pleased to hear bona fide verses proclaiming the glories of the Lord's holy names. We like to be reminded and encouraged to always chant and hear the holy names with great attention and devotion.

As a pure devotee of Lord Kṛṣṇa, King Kulaśekhara naturally worships the holy names of the Lord. Here he compares them to a medicine for curing the disease of *saṁsāra.* Of all dreaded maladies, *saṁsāra* is the worst, because it includes all other diseases. As long as we are bound to take birth in the material world, we must inevitably expose ourselves to cancers, heart attacks, AIDS, and so on. All cures within this world are temporary because even if we are cured of one disease, we will eventually contract another, either in the present life or a future one. As with our attempts for happiness, our attempts for health must fail sooner or later.

In previous ages in India, a criminal would sometimes be strapped to a chair and immersed in water almost to the point of drowning. Upon being brought up, he felt great relief—only to be plunged under again by his torturers. Similarly, the times when we are pain-free and happy are like the few seconds of relief the prisoner feels when he is brought up from under water. The basic principle of material life is suffering.

Therefore we should be very eager to receive the medicine that will cure all our diseases. The word *nirvāṇa* in this verse refers to the permanent cessation of *saṁsāra* and its attendant miseries. *Nirvāṇa* has become famous from the teachings of Buddhism, but the voidistic liberation the Buddhists teach is unnatural for the living entity, and thus it is temporary. We can find factual, permanent release from pain only in the kind of liberation King Kulaśekhara refers to here: the liberation of a devotee engaged in eternal service to the Supreme

Personality of Godhead. When through the process of devotional service we become free of all material desires and attain pure love of God, we will be transferred to the Vaikuṇṭha realm, where there are no anxieties or suffering.

At the beginning of the Tenth Canto of the *Śrīmad-Bhāgavatam* (10.1.4), King Parīkṣit also uses the word *auṣadhi* ("medicine") to refer to the chanting and hearing of *kṛṣṇa-kathā,* or words about Kṛṣṇa: "Descriptions of the Lord are the right medicine for the conditioned soul undergoing repeated birth and death." Such descriptions, of course, include the chanting and hearing of the Lord's holy name.

As with any bona fide medicine, one should take the nectarean potion of the holy name under the guidance of experts, in this case sages and the spiritual master. The Supreme Lord's names vary with His different pastimes and relationships with His pure devotees. He appeared as the son of Mother Yaśodā and also as the son of Mother Devakī, and therefore He is named Devakī-nandana and Yaśodā-nandana. One should receive the Lord's authorized names from the spiritual master in disciplic succession.

The *śāstras* recommend which names we should chant. For example, the *Kali-santaraṇa Upaniṣad* recommends the Hare Kṛṣṇa *mahā-mantra:* Hare Kṛṣṇa, Hare Kṛṣṇa, Kṛṣṇa Kṛṣṇa, Hare Hare/ Hare Rāma, Hare Rāma, Rāma Rāma, Hare Hare. We don't have to search for some name or manufacture one. Rather, we must follow the saintly persons and the *śāstras* in chanting the Lord's holy names, as Śrīla Prabhupāda recommends in his *Śrīmad-Bhāgavatam* (8.1.13, purport).

TEXT 16

हे मर्त्याः परमं हितं शृणुत वो वक्ष्यामि सङ्क्षेपतः
संसारार्णवमापदूर्मिबहुलं सम्यक् प्रविश्य स्थिताः ।
नानाज्ञानमपास्य चेतसि नमो नारायणायेत्यमुं
मन्त्रं सप्रणवं प्रणामसहितं प्रावर्तयध्वं मुहुः ॥१६॥

he martyāḥ paramaṁ hitaṁ śṛṇuta vo vakṣyāmi saṅkṣepataḥ
saṁsārārṇavam āpad-ūrmi-bahulaṁ samyak praviśya sthitāḥ
nānā-jñānam apāsya cetasi namo nārāyaṇāyety amuṁ
mantraṁ sa-praṇavaṁ praṇāma-sahitaṁ prāvartayadhvaṁ muhuḥ

he martyāḥ—O mortals; *paramam*—supreme; *hitam*—benefit; *śṛṇuta*—just hear about; *vaḥ*—to you; *vakṣyāmi*—I will tell; *saṅkṣepataḥ*—in summary; *saṁsāra*—of the cycle of material existence; *arṇavam*—the ocean; *āpat*—of misfortunes; *ūrmi*—with the waves; *bahulam*—crowded; *samyak*—fully; *praviśya*—having entered; *sthitāḥ*—situated within; *nānā*—various; *jñānam*—knowledge; *apāsya*—rejecting; *cetasi*—within your heart; *namaḥ*—obeisances; *nārāyaṇāya*—to Lord Nārāyaṇa; *iti*—thus; *amum*—this; *mantram*—chant; *sa-praṇavam*—together with the syllable *oṁ; praṇāma*—bowing down; *sahitam*—also with; *prāvartayadhvam*—please practice; *muhuḥ*—continuously.

TRANSLATION

O mortal beings, you have submerged yourselves fully in the ocean of material existence, which is filled with the waves of misfortune. Please hear as I briefly tell you how to attain your supreme benefit. Just put aside your various attempts at gaining knowledge and instead begin constantly chanting the *mantra oṁ namo nārāyaṇāya* and bowing down to the Lord.

PURPORT

No matter how expert a swimmer one may be, one cannot survive for long in a vast sea like the Pacific Ocean. Similarly, no matter how expert a materialist one may be, whether a *karmī, jñānī,* or *yogī,* one cannot survive forever amidst the tossing waves of *saṁsāra.* Indeed, all living entities are being tossed repeatedly from one life to the next, from one species to another. Many philosophers have sought relief from *saṁsāra* by cultivating knowledge, but no amount of mental speculation or Vedānta study will take one to the other shore of the ocean of *saṁsāra.* At best, a *jñānī* can come to know that all material life is suffering, and by further purification he can understand the spiritual oneness of all beings. But even that understainding does not bring ultimate relief. Liberation from the ocean of birth and death comes with direct surrender to the Supreme Lord, who personally frees the devotee from suffering. As Lord Kṛṣṇa states, "For the devotees I am the swift deliverer from the ocean of birth and death" (Bg. 12.7).

King Kulaśekhara recommends the constant chanting of God's names as the way out of *saṁsāra.* Of course, only one who has spontaneous love of God can continuously chant His holy names. Mechanical chanting cannot continue for very long. But even neophytes are advised to chant Hare Kṛṣṇa as much as possible to develop their taste for the holy names. A symptom of an advanced devotee is that he has *nāma-gāne sadā rucih,* tireless attraction for chanting or singing the Lord's names.

The six Gosvāmīs of Vṛndāvana achieved the perfect state of attraction for the holy names, chanting and hearing almost twenty-four hours daily. Prabhupāda writes, "Of course, we should not imitate him [Rūpa Gosvāmī], but the devotees of the Kṛṣṇa consciousness movement must at least be very careful to complete their sixteen rounds, their minimum amount of prescribed chanting. *Nāma-gāne sadā rucih:* we have to increase our taste for singing and chanting Hare Kṛṣṇa" (*Teachings of Queen Kuntī,* pp. 149–50).

Continuous chanting of the holy name with great relish (*ruci*) is the privilege of the advanced devotee, but one who chants with offenses is also recommended to chant constantly. As the *Padma Purāṇa* states, although in the beginning one may chant the Hare Kṛṣṇa *mantra* with offenses, one can free himself from those offenses by chanting again and again. *Pāpa-kṣayaś ca bhavati smaratāṁ tam ahar-niśam:* "One becomes free from all sinful reactions if one remembers the Lord day and night."

Whatever a person thinks of at the time of death determines his next life. This is another reason for chanting the holy names constantly. If we can chant at the difficult hour of death, we will guarantee our return home, back to Godhead, without a doubt.

TEXT 17

नाथे नः पुरुषोत्तमे त्रिजगतामेकाधिपे चेतसा
सेव्ये स्वस्य पदस्य दातरि परे नारायणे तिष्ठति ।
यं कञ्चित् पुरुषाधमं कतिपयग्रामेशमल्पार्थदं
सेवायै मृगयामहे नरमहो मूढा वराका वयम् ॥१७॥

nāthe naḥ puruṣottame tri-jagatām ekādhipe cetasā
sevye svasya padasya dātari pare nārāyaṇe tiṣṭhati
yaṁ kañcit puruṣādhamaṁ katipaya-grāmeśam alpārtha-daṁ
sevāyai mṛgayāmahe naram aho mūḍhā varākā vayam

nāthe—master; *naḥ*—our; *puruṣa-uttame*—the Personality of Godhead; *tri*—three; *jagatām*—of the worlds; *eka*—the one; *adhipe*—Lord; *cetasā*—by the mind; *sevye*—capable of being served; *svasya*—of His own; *padasya*—position; *dātari*—the granter; *pare*—the Supreme; *nārāyaṇe*—Lord Nārāyaṇa; *tiṣṭhati*—when He is present; *yam kañcit*—some; *puruṣa*—person; *adhamam*—lowly; *katipaya*—of a few; *grāma*—villages; *īśam*—controller; *alpa*—meager; *artha*—benefit; *dam*—who can give; *sevāyai*—for service; *mṛgayāmahe*—we seek out; *naram*—this man; *aho*—ah; *mūḍhāḥ*—bewildered; *varākāḥ*—degraded fools; *vayam*—we.

TRANSLATION

Our master, the Personality of Godhead Nārāyaṇa, who alone rules the three worlds, whom one can serve in meditation, and who happily shares His personal domain, is manifest before us. Yet still we beg for the service of some minor lord of a few villages, some lowly man who can only meagerly reward us. Alas, what foolish wretches we are!

PURPORT

The eternal *dharma* of the living being is to render service. No one can escape it. Originally we are meant to serve the Supreme Lord out of love, but in our conditioned state we forget the real object of service and out of selfish motives seek to serve unworthy masters. We serve such persons not out of love but in hopes of gaining remuneration from them. Even when we perform so-called altruistic acts, such service to country or humanity at large is usually tainted by a desire to be recognized as generous or compassionate. Ultimately, all materially motivated service is frustrated in many ways and winds up satisfying neither ourselves nor our masters.

By contrast, Kulaśekhara points out the great advantage of becoming the servant of the Supreme Lord. Lord Nārāyaṇa is the ruler of all the worlds (*sarva-loka-maheśvaram*). Part of His glory, however, is that although He is unlimitedly majestic and powerful, He makes Himself accessible so that we can easily serve Him anywhere and at any time by chanting His holy names or meditating on His form, qualities, pastimes, and instructions. Such devotional service should be performed without any desire for personal reward. But even if a conditioned soul harbors personal desires, he should render active service to the Supreme. As Śukadeva Gosvāmī said to King Parīkṣit in the *Śrīmad-Bhāgavatam* (2.3.10),

akāmaḥ sarva-kāmo vā mokṣa-kāma udāra-dhīḥ
tīvreṇa bhakti-yogena yajeta puruṣaṁ param

"A person who has broader intelligence, whether he be full of all material desire, without any material desire, or desiring liberation, must by all means worship the supreme whole, the Personality of Godhead."

Service to Lord Nārāyaṇa culminates in our rejoining Him in the eternal Vaikuṇṭha planets. There the servants of the Lord share almost equally in His opulences. As Śrīla Prabhupāda used to say, "Become great by serving the great." But despite the overwhelming advantages of serving Lord Nārāyaṇa, we still misdirect our service in the pitiful way King Kulaśekhara describes here.

Sometimes a person adopts the impersonal conception of the Absolute Truth and thinks that by practicing austerities and cultivating knowledge he will eventually become equal with the Supreme in all respects: "I will give up serving and become the Self," he thinks. This resistance to *bhakti* results from ignorance of the transcendental pleasure the Lord's servant enjoys. If we actually knew how happy we would become by acting in our constitutional position as the Lord's servant, we would take up devotional service at once.

In this connection, Śrīla Prabhupāda tells the story of a man whose burning desire was to serve the greatest person. The man was born into a small village, where he became attracted to serving the village chief. He was very happy in this capacity and tried to please the chief in many ways. But one day a district governor visited the village, and the servant came to understand that his local chief was also a servant—of the governor. He then asked to be transferred to the service of the greater master. The governor accepted him into his service, and the man was again satisfied trying to please his new master. But then he saw that the governor was paying taxes and offering obeisances to the king. The man who wanted to serve the greatest managed to transfer himself into the king's direct service. Now he was completely satisfied, and the king treated him as a favorite servant. But one day the man saw that the king went off alone into the woods to worship and serve an ascetic. The king's servant later approached that *guru* and addressed him, "You must be the greatest person of all, because even the king serves you. Please let me be your servant." The ascetic replied that he himself was the lowly servant of the Supreme Personality of Godhead, Kṛṣṇa. The perpetual servant then asked where he could find Kṛṣṇa, and the *guru* directed him to the nearest Kṛṣṇa temple. With an ardent desire the servant went to the temple and received a direct indication from the Deity that he was indeed accepted as His servant. Finally, the aspiring servant of the greatest reached his goal, a position as the servant of the Supreme Personality of Godhead.

There are five major *rasas,* or relationships, with the Supreme Lord, but the basis of them all is service. The glories of loving service won praise from the great *yogī* Durvāsā Muni, who saw how pleased the Supreme Lord was with His pure devotee Ambarīṣa. Durvāsā said, "What remains to be attained for those who have become the Lord's servants?" And in the *Stotra-ratna* (43), Śrī Yāmunācārya states,

bhavantam evānucaran nirantaraḥ
praśānta-niḥśeṣa-mano-rathāntaraḥ
kadāham aikāntika-nitya-kiṅkaraḥ
praharṣayiṣyāmi sanātha-jīvitam

"By serving You constantly, one is freed from all material desires and is completely pacified. When shall I engage as Your permanent eternal servant and always feel joyful to have such a perfect master?" (Cc. *Madhya* 1.206).

Another reason a foolish *jīva* may avoid serving the Lord is because of social pressure. If we serve Lord Kṛṣṇa, many people may laugh at us, whereas if we serve the mundane gods of money, prestige, and power, we will be widely accepted. Some people prefer to seek anonymity, and they are afraid that becoming a devotee of the Lord would make them far too noticeable. A real devotee, however, derives such great satisfaction from his service to the spiritual master and Kṛṣṇa that he doesn't care what others think. As the *Śrīmad-Bhāgavatam* (11.2.40) states,

evaṁ-vrataḥ sva-priya-nāma-kīrtyā
jātānurāgo druta-citta uccaiḥ
hasaty atho roditi rauti gāyaty
unmāda-van nṛtyati loka-bāhyaḥ

"By chanting the holy name of the Lord, one comes to the stage of love of Godhead. Then the devotee is fixed in his vow as an eternal servant of the Lord, and he gradually becomes very much attached to a particular name and form of the Lord. As his heart melts with ecstatic love, he laughs very loudly or cries and shouts. Sometimes he sings and dances like a madman, for he is indifferent to public opinion."

Devotees in the Kṛṣṇa consciousness movement may be shy at first, but they soon learn to forget their inhibitions while publicly chanting the holy names and dancing. They do this as a service to the Lord, for the welfare of all people, and they also find it ecstatic. In his *Padyāvalī* (73), Śrīla Rūpa Gosvāmī quotes a verse written by Sārvabhauma Bhaṭṭācārya describing just how ecstatic devotional service can be, and how indifferent to public opinion an ecstatic devotee is: "Let the garrulous populace say whatever they like. We shall pay them no regard. Thoroughly maddened by the ecstasy of the intoxicating beverage of love for Kṛṣṇa, we shall enjoy life, running about and rolling on the ground and dancing in ecstasy."

TEXT 18

बद्धेनाञ्जलिना नतेन शिरसा गात्रैः सरोमोद्गमैः
कण्ठेन स्वरगद्गदेन नयनेनोद्गीर्णबाष्पाम्बुना ।
नित्यं त्वच्चरणारविन्दयुगलध्यानामृतास्वादिनाम्
अस्माकं सरसीरुहाक्ष सततं सम्पद्यतां जीवितम् ॥१८॥

baddhenāñjalinā natena śirasā gātraiḥ sa-romodgamaiḥ
kaṇṭhena svara-gadgadena nayanenodgīrṇa-bāṣpāmbunā
nityaṁ tvac-caraṇāravinda-yugala-dhyānāmṛtāsvādinām
asmākaṁ sarasīruhākṣa satataṁ sampadyatāṁ jīvitam

baddhena—closed together; *añjalinā*—with joined palms; *natena*—bowed down; *śirasā*—with our heads; *gātraiḥ*—with bodily limbs; *sa*—having; *roma*—of their hair; *udgamaiḥ*—eruptions; *kaṇṭhena*—with the voice; *svara*—sounds; *gadgadena*—choked up; *nayanena*—with eyes; *udgīrṇa*—emitting; *bāṣpa*—of tears; *ambunā*—with the water; *nityam*—constant; *tvat*—Your; *caraṇa*—of the feet; *aravinda*—lotus; *yugala*—on the pair; *dhyāna*—from meditation; *amṛta*—immortal nectar;

āsvādinām—who are tasting; *asmākam*—our; *sarasī-ruha*—like a lotus growing in a lake; *akṣa*—O You whose eyes; *satatam*—always; *sampadyatām*—please assure; *jīvitam*—our livelihood.

TRANSLATION

O lotus-eyed Lord, please sustain our lives as we constantly relish the nectar of meditating on Your lotus feet, with our palms prayerfully joined, our heads bowed down, our bodily hair standing up in jubilation, our voices choked with emotion, and our eyes flowing with tears.

PURPORT

A devotee finds full satisaction in reverently worshiping his Lord, appreciating His personal features. And while rapt in worshiping the Lord, a Vaiṣṇava does not worry much about his own sustenance. In modern cities, by contrast, earning one's livelihood has become an exaggerated endeavor that takes one's full energy, day and night, leaving no time left for God, except perhaps on Sunday, the day of rest.

The Vedic philosophy teaches that the top priority in life should be reawakening our relationship with the Lord. Therefore a sensible man should never allow himself to get so wrapped up in his material duties that they sap all his energy and kill his desire for serving Kṛṣṇa. Śrīla Bhaktivinoda Ṭhākura, who was both a great Vaiṣṇava and a responsible magistrate in the Indian government, said that we should balance our material and spiritual needs, but that we should favor the latter. In other words, we should earn our livelihood in the spirit of simple living and high thinking.

In the *Śrīmad-Bhāgavatam* (7.14.6), Nārada Muni recommends just such a life to Mahārāja Yudhiṣṭhira: "An intelligent man in human society should make his program of activities very simple. If there are suggestions from his friends, children, parents, brothers, or anyone else, he should externally agree, saying, 'Yes, that is all right,' but internally he should be determined not to create a cumbersome life in which the purpose of life will not be fulfilled."

An ideal service for a householder is Deity worship, either at home or in the temple. As one cleans the altar, cooks, or dresses the Deity, one should relish the nectar of meditating on the Lord's lotus feet, as King Kulaśekhara says in this prayer. To be effective, worship must never be done in a time-serving mood. Sometimes Māyāvādīs appear to worship Deities as the Vaiṣṇavas do. But there is a world of difference, because Māyāvādīs do not think that the Supreme Lord is a perpetual object of devotion. Rather, they think that Deity worship may help one develop a meditative mood, which will eventually lead one to realize that the Lord Himself is illusion. Then the worshiper merges with the impersonal Brahman. Neither the Supreme Lord nor His pure devotee ever accepts this kind of time-serving *bhakti*.

The *Śrīmad-Bhagavatam* and all the spiritual masters in disciplic succession warn us never to consider Deity worship to be idol worship. The *arcā-vigraha* is not a symbolic creation but is Kṛṣṇa Himself appearing in a form of metal, stone, wood, etc., to facilitate devotional exchanges with His devotees.

One of the great blessings of Deity worship is that it provides us with a concrete image to meditate on. Thus Deity worship, in conjunction with descriptions of the Lord found in authorized *śāstras* like *Śrīmad-Bhāgavatam,* enables the devotee easily to absorb his mind in the form of the Lord. Here are just two of the many descriptions of the Lord's form found in the *Bhāgavatam:*

"His lotus feet are placed over the whorls of the lotuslike hearts of great mystics. On His chest is the Kaustubha jewel, engraved with a beautiful calf, and there are other jewels on His shoulders. His complete torso is garlanded with fresh flowers" (*Bhāg.* 2.2.10).

"Kṛṣṇa's face is decorated with ornaments, such as earrings resembling sharks. His ears are beautiful, His cheeks are brilliant, and His smiling face is attractive to everyone. Whoever sees Lord Kṛṣṇa sees a festival. His face and body are fully satisfying for everyone to see, but the devotees are angry at the creator for the disturbance caused by the momentary blinking of their eyes" (*Bhāg.* 9.24.65).

TEXT 19

यत्कृष्णप्रणिपातधूलिधवलं तद्वर्ष्म तद्वै शिरस्
ते नेत्रे तमसोज्झिते सुरुचिरे याभ्यां हरिर्दृश्यते ।
सा बुद्धिर्विमलेन्दुशङ्खधवला या माधवध्यायिनी
सा जिह्वामृतवर्षिणी प्रतिपदं या स्तौति नारायणम् ॥१९॥

yat kṛṣṇa-praṇipāta-dhūli-dhavalaṁ tad varṣma tad vai śiras
te netre tamasojjhite su-rucire yābhyāṁ harir dṛśyate
sā buddhir vimalendu-śaṅkha-dhavalā yā mādhava-dhyāyinī
sā jihvāmṛta-varṣiṇī prati-padaṁ yā stauti nārāyaṇam

yat—which; *kṛṣṇa*—to Lord Kṛṣṇa; *praṇipāta*—from bowing down; *dhūli*—with dust; *dhavalam*—whitened; *tat*—that; *varṣma*—topmost; *tat*—that; *vai*—indeed; *śiraḥ*—head; *te*—those two; *netre*—eyes; *tamasā*—by darkness; *ujjhite*—abandoned; *su*—very; *rucire*—attractive; *yābhyām*—by which; *hariḥ*—Lord Hari; *dṛśyate*—is seen; *sā*—that; *buddhiḥ*—intelligence; *vimalā*—spotless; *indu*—like the moon; *śaṅkha*—or a conchshell; *dhavalā*—shining white; *yā*—which; *mādhava-dhyāyanī*—meditating on Lord Mādhava; *sā*—that; *jihvā*—tongue; *amṛta*—nectar; *varṣiṇī*—raining down; *prati-padam*—at every step; *yā*—which; *stauti*—praises; *nārāyaṇam*—Lord Nārāyaṇa.

TRANSLATION

That head is the loftiest which is white with dust from bowing down to Lord Kṛṣṇa. Those eyes are the most beautiful which darkness has abandoned after they have seen Lord Hari. That intelligence is spotless—like the white glow of the moon or a conchshell—which concentrates on Lord Mādhava. And that tongue rains down nectar which constantly glorifies Lord Nārāyaṇa.

PURPORT

Devotional service to Lord Kṛṣṇa gradually spiritualizes and beautifies all one's senses. Ordinary people may not see how a Vaiṣṇava is being transformed, for only a devotee can appreciate the actual beauty of other devotees. Therefore Śrīla Rūpa Gosvāmī cautions us in his *Upadeśāmṛta* (5) against judging a devotee superficially: "One should overlook a devotee's being born in a low family, having a body with a bad complexion, a deformed body, or a diseased or infirm body. According to ordinary vision, such imperfections may seem prominent in the body of a pure devotee, but despite such seeming defects, the body of a pure devotee cannot be polluted. It is exactly like the waters of the Ganges, which during the rainy season are sometimes full of bubbles, foam, and mud [but which remain pure and thus able to purify one who bathes in them]."

Often, however, the transforming power of devotional service is dramatic. Śrīla Prabhupāda would sometimes recall how when he first met many of his future disciples, they were dirty, morose hippies. But as they took to Kṛṣṇa consciousness, Prabhupāda said, they became like bright-faced angels from Vaikuṇṭha.

In the course of the Lord's pastimes, the Lord will sometimes personally cause dramatic changes in His devotees' bodies. As Lord Kṛṣṇa entered Mathurā He met a young hunchback girl who anointed Him with sandalwood pulp that had been meant for King Kaṁsa, and in return for her service the Lord straightened her body and changed her into a beautiful girl. Similarly, Lord Caitanya instantly cured the leper Vāsudeva. The ultimate bodily transformation takes place when a devotee gains his *svarūpa,* his spiritual body, and enters the spiritual world to worship the Lord in Vaikuṇṭha.

A devotee becomes beautiful by humbling himself in the dust as he offers obeisances to the Lord. By contrast, a proud person who is trying to impress the opposite sex with his or her so-called beauty will avoid bowing in the dust. But King Kulaśekhara recommends it as a kind of beauty treatment. True beauty means that which is pleasing to Lord Kṛṣṇa.

The devotees' eyes become beautiful by seeing the most beautiful form of Kṛṣṇa. A reflection of Kṛṣṇa's radiance shines in the eyes of devotional mystics. Those who saw His Divine Grace Śrīla Prabhupāda saw this radiance in his eyes.

The spotless intelligence referred to here is one that is cleansed of all doubts and filled with pure faith in the Lord. One who has attained such clear *buddhi,* spiritual intelligence, is peaceful and is able to solve all problems, both his own and others'. Therefore the devotees' intelligence is likened to the moon, whose cool, soothing beauty can be seen and appreciated by everyone in the world. Similarly, the tongue of one who glorifies the Lord is said to shower down a rain of nectar, which, like the moonshine, is available to all without distinction.

TEXT 20

जिह्वे कीर्तय केशवं मुररिपुं चेतो भज श्रीधरं
पाणिद्वन्द्व समर्चयाच्युतकथाः श्रोत्रद्वय त्वं शृणु ।

कृष्णं लोकय लोचनद्वय हरेर्गच्छांघ्रियुग्मालयं
जिघ्र घ्राण मुकुन्दपादतुलसीं मूर्धन्नमाधोक्षजम् ॥२०॥

jihve kīrtaya keśavaṁ mura-ripuṁ ceto bhaja śrīdharaṁ
pāṇi-dvandva samarcayācyuta-kathāḥ śrotra-dvaya tvaṁ śṛṇu
kṛṣṇaṁ lokaya locana-dvaya harer gacchāṅghri-yugmālayaṁ
jighra ghrāṇa mukunda-pāda-tulasīṁ mūrdhan namādhokṣajam

jihve—O tongue; *kīrtaya*—chant the praise; *keśavam*—of Lord Keśava; *mura-ripum*—the enemy of Mura; *cetaḥ*—O mind; *bhaja*—worship; *śrī-dharam*—the Lord of Śrī, the goddess of fortune; *pāṇi-dvandva*—O two hands; *samarcaya*—serve; *acyuta-kathāḥ*—topics of Lord Acyuta; *śrotra-dvaya*—O two ears; *tvam*—you; *śṛṇu*—just hear; *kṛṣṇam*—at Kṛṣṇa; *lokaya*—look; *locana-dvaya*—O two eyes; *hareḥ*—of Lord Hari; *gaccha*—go to; *aṅghri-yugma*—O two feet; *ālayam*—to the residence; *jighra*—smell; *ghrāṇa*—O nose; *mukunda*—of Lord Mukunda; *pāda*—at the feet; *tulasīm*—the *tulasī* flowers; *mūrdhan*—O head; *nama*—bow down; *adhokṣajam*—to Lord Adhokṣaja.

TRANSLATION

O tongue, praise the glories of Lord Keśava. O mind, worship the enemy of Mura. O hands, serve the Lord of Śrī. O ears, hear the topics of Lord Acyuta. O eyes, gaze upon Śrī Kṛṣṇa. O feet, go to the temple of Lord Hari. O nose, smell the *tulasī* buds on Lord Mukunda's feet. O head, bow down to Lord Adhokṣaja.

PURPORT

Here the poet orders each of his senses to cooperate in serving the Lord. The spirit soul is higher than the senses, and so it is right that he should order them:

indriyāni parāṇy āhur indriyebyaḥ paraṁ manaḥ
manasas tu parā buddhir yo buddheḥ paratas tu saḥ

"The working senses are superior to dull matter; mind is higher than the senses; intelligence is still higher than the mind; and he [the soul] is even higher than the intelligence" (Bg. 3.42).

Texts 19 and 20 of *Mukunda-mālā-stotra* call to mind a series of verses by Śaunaka Ṛṣi in *Śrīmad-Bhāgavatam* (2.3.20–24): "One who has not listened to the messages about the prowess and marvelous acts of the Personality of Godhead and has not sung or chanted loudly the worthy songs about the Lord is to be considered to possess earholes like the holes snakes live in and a tongue like the tongue of a frog. The upper portion of the body, though crowned with a silk turban, is only a heavy burden if not bowed down before the Personality of Godhead, who can award *mukti* [freedom from birth and death]. And the hands, though decorated with glittering bangles, are like those of a dead man if not engaged in the service of the Personality of Godhead, Hari. The eyes which do not look at the symbolic representations [Deity forms] of the Personality of Godhead, Viṣṇu, are like those printed on the plumes of the peacock, and the legs which do not move to the holy places [where the Lord is remembered] are considered to be like tree trunks. The person who has not at any time received the dust of the feet of the Lord's pure devotee upon his head is certainly a dead body. And the person who has never experienced the aroma of the *tulasī* flowers decorating the lotus feet of the Lord is also a dead body, although breathing. Certainly that heart is steel-framed which, in spite of one's chanting the holy name of the Lord with concentration, does not change and feel ecstasy, at which time tears fill the eyes and the hairs stand on end."

Each of our senses may help or hinder us in devotional service. If we allow even one sense free rein, it can seriously distract our mind, just as a gust of wind can sweep away an unanchored sailboat on the ocean. The Supreme Personality of Godhead has senses, and so do we, and our perfection lies in serving Hṛṣīkeśa (the Lord of the senses) with all of our senses. We may engage our senses in the service of Kṛṣṇa or in the service of Māyā, illusion. The choice is vividly shown in the verses by Kulaśekhara and Śaunaka Ṛṣi.

For example, our sincere singing (*kīrtana*) may please the Supreme Lord and evoke His mercy, or our materialistic songs will resemble the frog's croaking, which attracts the predator snake—death. Similarly, we may be beautified by bowing our head before the Lord, or that same head, burdened by ornaments and pride, will drag us down into the ocean of birth and death. A person in a high social position is often too proud to humble himself before the Deity in the temple. In that case he will be pulled down by his own pride, just as a man who falls overboard in the ocean is pulled down by his heavy clothes and headdress. In Lord Caitanya's time, King Pratāparudra set the perfect example for a worldly leader by performing the menial service of sweeping the road before Lord Jagannātha's chariot. In this way he showed his subordination to the Almighty.

One can best serve the Lord's senses by serving His devotees. Śrīla Prabhupāda states, "Kṛṣṇa is the property of His pure, unconditioned devotees, and as such only the devotees can deliver Kṛṣṇa to another devotee; Kṛṣṇa is never obtainable directly" (*Bhāg.* 2.3.23, purport). A disciple should therefore use his senses to perform all kinds of services for the satisfaction of his *guru.*

We should engage not only our senses but also our mind in the Lord's service. The mind, after all, provides the impetus for the actions of all the bodily limbs. So thinking of Kṛṣṇa is the basis of all devotional service. As the Lord instructs in the *Bhagavad-gītā* (9.34), *man-manā bhava mad-bhaktaḥ:* "Think of Me and become My devotee." The mind fixed in chanting and praying to Kṛṣṇa will change the heart, which will transform the conditioned soul into a pure devotee. A pure devotee, therefore, is one whose body, mind, and words are all merged in devotional service to Kṛṣṇa, with no room for illusion.

TEXT 21

आम्नायाभ्यसनान्यरण्यरुदितं वेदव्रतान्यन्वहं
मेदश्छेदफलानि पूर्तविधयः सर्वं हुतं भस्मनि ।
तीर्थानामवगाहनानि च गजस्नानं विना यत्पद-
द्वन्द्वाम्भोरुहसंस्मृतिं विजयते देवः स नारायणः ॥२१॥

āmnāyābhyasanāny araṇya-ruditaṁ veda-vratāny anv-ahaṁ
medaś-cheda-phalāni pūrta-vidhayaḥ sarvaṁ hutaṁ bhasmani
tīrthānām avagāhanāni ca gaja-snānaṁ vinā yat-pada-
dvandvāmbhoruha-saṁsmṛtiṁ vijayate devaḥ sa nārāyaṇaḥ

āmnāya—of the revealed scriptures; *abhyasanāni*—studies; *araṇya*—

in the forest; *ruditam*—crying; *veda*—Vedic; *vratāni*—vows of austerity; *anu-aham*—daily; *medaḥ*—of fat; *cheda*—removal; *phalāni*—whose result; *pūrta-vidhayaḥ*—prescribed pious works; *sarvam*—all; *hutam*—oblations offered; *bhasmani*—onto ashes; *tīrthānām*—at holy sites; *avagāhanāni*—acts of bathing; *ca*—and; *gaja*—of an elephant; *snānam*—the bathing; *vinā*—without; *yat*—whose; *pada*—of the feet; *dvandva*—the pair; *amboruha*—lotus; *saṁsmṛtim*—remembrance; *vijayate*—may He be victorious; *devaḥ*—the Lord; *saḥ*—He; *nārāyaṇaḥ*—Nārāyaṇa.

TRANSLATION

All glories to Lord Nārāyaṇa! Without remembrance of His lotus feet, recitation of scripture is merely crying in the wilderness, regular observance of severe vows enjoined in the *Vedas* is no more than a way to lose weight, execution of prescribed pious duties is like pouring oblations onto ashes, and bathing at various holy sites is no better than an elephant's bath.

PURPORT

Remembrance of the Supreme Personality of Godhead is the goal of all spiritual practices. One moment's remembrance of Lord Kṛṣṇa is the greatest fortune, and a moment's forgetfulness of Him is the greatest loss. Therefore even the important religious duties mentioned in this verse become null and void if they do not lead to remembrance of Kṛṣṇa. Studying the scriptures, visiting temples, observing vows—none of these is unimportant or dispensable for devotees. King Kulaśekhara, therefore, condemns them only when they are improperly performed in the name of religion. For example, the studies and meditations of the impersonalists, who deride the personal, spiritual form of the Absolute Truth, are useless. Other useless acts would include austerities performed for political ends or demigod worship aimed at winning material boons. The renunciant may become very skinny, but he will not please the Lord, and therefore he himself will not be pleased at heart. So what is the use of his austerities? As stated in the *Nārada-pañcarātra:*

ārādhito yadi haris tapasā tataḥ kim
nārādhito yadi haris tapasā tataḥ kim

antar bahir yadi haris tapasā tataḥ kim
nāntar bahir yadi haris tapasā tataḥ kim

"If one is worshiping Lord Hari, what is the use of severe penances? And if one is not worshiping Lord Hari, what is the use of severe penances? If one can understand that Lord Hari is all-pervading, what is the use of severe penances? And if one cannot understand that Lord Hari is all-pervading, what is the use of severe penances?"

The successful devotee has learned to think of the Lord in every conceivable circumstance. Thinking of Kṛṣṇa is not something to be practiced only when we are removed from our daily occupation, as in solitary meditation. Rather, Lord Kṛṣṇa instructed Arjuna to "remember Me and fight." In other words, we are meant to carry out our daily duties and at the same time think of Kṛṣṇa. Lord Caitanya's injunction to always chant the names of Kṛṣṇa is the same instruction, given in such a way that we can happily and easily follow it. In the advanced stage, a devotee effortlessly remembers Kṛṣṇa out of spontaneous love. In the beginning and intermediate stages, one can also think of Kṛṣṇa day and night, by chanting the holy name and molding one's activities in His service, under the direction of a pure devotee of the Lord.

TEXT 22

मदन परिहर स्थितिं मदीये
मनसि मुकुन्दपदारविन्दधाम्नि ।
हरनयनकृशानुना कृशोऽसि
स्मरसि न चक्रपराक्रमं मुरारेः ॥२२॥

madana parihara sthitiṁ madīye
manasi mukunda-padāravinda-dhāmni
hara-nayana-kṛśānunā kṛśo 'si
smarasi na cakra-parākramaṁ murāreḥ

madana—O Cupid; *parihara*—give up; *sthitim*—your residence; *madīye*—my; *manasi*—in the mind; *mukunda*—of Lord Mukunda; *pada-aravinda*—of the lotus feet; *dhāmni*—which is the abode; *hara*—of Lord Śiva; *nayana*—from the eye; *kṛśānunā*—by the fire; *kṛśaḥ*—decimated; *asi*—you have become; *smarasi na*—you do not remember; *cakra*—of the disc weapon; *parākramam*—the powerful capability; *mura-areḥ*—of the enemy of Mura.

TRANSLATION

O Cupid, abandon your residence in my mind, which is now the home of Lord Mukunda's lotus feet. You have already been incinerated by Lord Śiva's fiery glance, so why have you forgotten the power of Lord Murāri's disc?

PURPORT

This is a bold challenge to Cupid, who can usually subdue everyone, including aspiring transcendentalists. As Lord Kapila says to His mother, "Just try to understand the mighty strength of My *māyā* in the shape of a woman, who by the mere movement of her eyebrows can keep even the greatest conquerors of the world under her grip" (*Bhāg.* 3.31.38).

A devotee can challenge Kāmadeva (Cupid) in such a feisty way because devotees constantly meditate on Lord Kṛṣṇa, who destroys Cupid's influence. Here King Kulaśekhara is giving fair warning to Kāmadeva to leave the king's mind or risk destruction for a second time. The reference here is to an incident in which Kāmadeva tried to shoot his arrows at Lord Śiva to arouse lust in him. Lord Śiva retaliated by burning Kāmadeva to ashes with his glance. Kāmadeva should have learned his lesson from that incident. If not, King Kulaśekhara warns that Lord Kṛṣṇa will have no trouble destroying Kāmadeva with His disc and freeing His devotee's mind of lust.

Kāmadeva is also called Madana, a name that means "one who attracts." But Lord Kṛṣṇa is known as Madana-mohana, "the bewilderer of Cupid." In other words, Kṛṣṇa is so transcendentally attractive that anyone who absorbs his mind in Him will not be troubled by sex desire. Furthermore, Lord Kṛṣṇa's consort, Śrīmatī Rādhārāṇī, is called Madana-mohana-mohinī because She alone can captivate even Kṛṣṇa.

In all the world's religions, ascetics have practiced renunciation, and Kāmadeva always tests them and gives them trouble. Often, despite one's best attempts at purification, one thinks of the opposite sex at the time of death. Then one has to come back in the cycle of birth and death, to be again attracted and again suffer the miseries of material life. Even the powerful mystic Viśvāmitra became a victim of the beauty of Menakā, united with her, and begot Śakuntalā.

But the *bhaktas* have discovered an infallible shelter from Cupid—absorption in the beauty of Kṛṣṇa. One who is captivated by the beauty of Kṛṣṇa is not victimized by lust. As Śrī Yāmunācārya sings,

yad-avadhi mama cetaḥ kṛṣṇa-pādāravinde
nava-nava-rasa-dhāmany udyataṁ rantum āsīt
tad-avadhi bata nārī-saṅgame smaryamāne
bhavati mukha-vikāraḥ suṣṭhu niṣṭhīvanaṁ ca

"Since my mind has been engaged in the service of the lotus feet of Lord Kṛṣṇa and I have been enjoying ever-new transcendental pleasure in that service, whenever I think of sex with a woman my face at once turns from it, and I spit at the thought."

TEXT 23

नाथे धातरि भोगिभोगशयने नारायणे माधवे
देवे देवकिनन्दने सुरवरे चक्रायुधे शार्ङ्गिणि ।
लीलाशेषजगत्प्रपञ्चजठरे विश्वेश्वरे श्रीधरे
गोविन्दे कुरु चित्तवृत्तिमचलामन्यैस्तु किं वर्तनैः ॥२३॥

nāthe dhātari bhogi-bhoga-śayane nārāyaṇe mādhave
deve devaki-nandane sura-vare cakrāyudhe śārṅgiṇi
līlāśeṣa-jagat-prapañca-jaṭhare viśveśvare śrīdhare
govinde kuru citta-vṛttim acalām anyais tu kiṁ vartanaiḥ

nāthe—on your master; *dhātari*—and sustainer; *bhogi*—of the serpent (Ananta Śeṣa); *bhoga*—on the body; *śayane*—who lies down; *nārāyaṇe mādhave*—known as Nārāyaṇa and Mādhava; *deve*—the Supreme Lord; *devaki-nandane*—the darling son of Devakī; *sura-vare*—the hero of the demigods; *cakra-āyudhe*—the holder of the disc; *śārṅgiṇi*—the possessor of the bow Śārṅga; *līlā*—as a pastime; *aśeṣa*—endless; *jagat*—universes; *prapañca*—manifestation; *jaṭhare*—in the stomach; *viśva*—of the universes; *īśvare*—the controller; *śrīdhare*—the Lord of Śrī; *govinde*—on Lord Govinda; *kuru*—place; *citta*—of your mind; *vṛttim*—the workings; *acalām*—without deviation; *anyaiḥ*—other; *tu*—conversely; *kim*—what is the use; *vartanaiḥ*—with engagements.

TRANSLATION

Think only of your master and sustainer, the Supreme Lord, who is known as Nārāyaṇa and Mādhava and who lies on the body of the serpent Ananta. He is the darling son of Devakī, the hero of the demigods, and the Lord of the cows, and He holds a conchshell and the bow Śārṅga. He is the husband of the goddess of fortune and the controller of all the universes, which He manifests from His abdomen as a pastime. What will you gain by thinking of anything else?

PURPORT

In previous verses King Kulaśekhara has instructed his own mind to be fixed at the lotus feet of Kṛṣṇa, and now he instructs his readers to fix their minds on Him as well. He gives some of the Lord's innumerable names, which describe His qualities and pastimes. Devotees are attracted to serving a specific aspect of the Supreme Lord according to their specific *rasa,* or loving relationship with Him. One may meditate on and serve any bona fide form of the Lord and derive the same benefit of going back to Godhead. While passing away from the world, Grandfather Bhīṣma, who was in a chivalrous relationship with Kṛṣṇa, chanted prayers recalling that aspect of the Lord. Praying that his mind would go unto Kṛṣṇa, he reviewed the Lord's chivalrous pastimes in his mind: "May He, Lord Śrī Kṛṣṇa, the Personality of Godhead, who awards salvation, be my ultimte destination. On the battlefield He charged me, as if angry because of the wounds dealt by my sharp arrows. His shield was scattered, and His body was smeared with blood due to the wounds" (*Bhāg.* 1.9.38).

In this verse King Kulaśekhara instructs us to attain *samādhi,* or ecstatic concentration on the Supreme. *Yogīs* try to achieve *samādhi* by perfecting the eightfold *yoga* process, but this is very difficult. When Kṛṣṇa recommended this practice to Arjuna, he replied, "O Madhusūdana, the system of *yoga* You have summarized appears impractical and unbearable to me, for the mind is restless and unsteady. . . . [Controlling the mind] is more difficult than controlling the wind" (Bg. 6.33–34).

By contrast, *bhakti-yoga* is so easy that anyone can successfully practice it. A sincere soul who chants and hears the holy names of Kṛṣṇa, and also hears His pastimes and qualities narrated by self-realized devotees, can progress to the highest stages of concentration with an ease unknown to the followers of other *yoga* processes.

Why does King Kulaśekhara deem as worthless all activities except fixing the mind on Kṛṣṇa? Because all other acts and thoughts are temporary and thus lead to unending entanglement in material misery. As Śrīla Prabhupāda writes in his *Bhagavad-gītā* commentary, "If one is not in Krsna consciousness, there cannot be a final goal for the mind." By the tricks of fate and the inexorable workings of *karma,* what appears auspicious and happy one moment may turn into tragedy the next. Like the Supreme Lord, the soul is *sac-cid-ānanda-vigraha* (eternal and full of bliss and knowledge), and as such he can be fully satisfied only when he unites in *bhakti* with the Lord. We should join with Bhīṣmadeva in praying, "May His lotus feet always remain the objects of my attraction."

TEXT 24

मा द्राक्षं क्षीणपुण्यान् क्षणमपि भवतो भक्तिहीनान् पदाब्जे
मा श्रौषं श्राव्यबन्धं तव चरितमपास्यान्यदाख्यानजातम् ।
मा स्मार्षं माधव त्वामपि भुवनपते चेतसापह्नुवानान्
मा भूवं त्वत्सपर्याव्यतिकररहितो जन्मजन्मान्तरेऽपि ॥२४॥

mā drākṣaṁ kṣīṇa-puṇyān kṣaṇam api bhavato bhakti-hīnān padābje
mā śrauṣaṁ śrāvya-bandhaṁ tava caritam apāsyānyad ākhyāna-jātam
mā smārṣaṁ mādhava tvām api bhuvana-pate cetasāpahnuvānān
mā bhūvaṁ tvat-saparyā-vyatikara-rahito janma-janmāntare 'pi

mā drākṣam—may I not look at; *kṣīṇa*—depleted; *puṇyān*—whose credit of piety; *kṣaṇam*—a moment; *api*—even; *bhavataḥ*—Your; *bhakti*—devotion; *hīnān*—devoid of; *pada-abje*—for the lotus feet; *mā śrauṣam*—may I not hear; *śrāvya*—worth hearing; *bandham*—compositions about which; *tava*—Your; *caritam*—pastimes; *apāsya*—putting aside; *anyat*—other; *ākhyāna*—of narrations; *jātam*—topics; *mā śmārṣam*—may I not remember; *mādhava*—O Mādhava; *tvām*—Your; *api*—indeed; *bhuvana*—of the world; *pate*—O master; *cetasā*—mentally; *apahnuvānān*—those who avoid; *mā bhūvam*—may I not become; *tvat*—Your; *saparyā*—for the personal service; *vyatikara*—the opportunity; *rahitaḥ*—devoid of; *janma-janma-antare*—in repeated rebirths; *api*—even.

TRANSLATION

O Mādhava, please do not let me even glance at those whose pious credits are so depleted that they have no devotion for Your lotus feet. Please do not let me be distracted from listening to the worthy narrations of Your pastimes and become interested in other topics. Please, O Lord of the universe, let me pay no attention to those who avoid thinking of You. And let me never be unable to serve You in some menial way, birth after birth.

PURPORT

Like other Vaiṣṇavas' prayers, King Kulaśekhara's are characterized by single-minded intensity. A critic might say his attitude doesn't embody the "golden mean" praised in Greek wisdom. The critic might ask, "What's wrong with sometimes serving Kṛṣṇa and sometimes enjoying yourself in sense gratification? Why be so fanatical as to avoid even glancing at impious persons? And why focus exclusively on the Deity of Lord Viṣṇu?" These questions are not to be answered by reason alone. The devotee's exclusive intensity is dictated by love. It is unreasonable to ask someone in love to be interested in something other than his beloved.

But *kṛṣṇa-bhakti* is not an ordinary lover's madness. Śrī Kṛṣṇa is the Absolute Truth, the source of supreme wisdom, and, as such, in the *Bhagavad-gītā* He teaches single-minded devotion to Himself:

bhaktyā tv ananyayā śakya aham evaṁ-vidho 'rjuna
jñātuṁ draṣṭuṁ ca tattvena praveṣṭuṁ ca parantapa

"My dear Arjuna, only by undivided devotional service can I be understood as I am, standing before you, and can thus be seen directly. Only in this way can you enter into the mysteries of My understanding" (Bg. 11.54). Furthermore, unlike ordinary, materialistic "love," one-pointed devotion to Kṛṣṇa does not produce indifference to everyone else besides one's beloved. While in this verse King Kulaśekhara expresses his valid wish to avoid the association of nondevotees, out of compassion a pure devotee will "glance at" and "pay attention to" nondevotees for the sake of preaching.

When a devotee actually becomes fully absorbed in Kṛṣṇa, he sees the whole world as the Lord's creation and everything as part and parcel of His energies. Through his exclusive devotion to the Lord, the devotee becomes a *mahātmā,* a high-souled person who works for the benefit of all living beings by reminding them of their connection with Kṛṣṇa.

The stage of Kṛṣṇa consciousness King Kulaśekhara desires is not artificial but is the original state of the living being. He is therefore calling out to the Lord to invoke His mercy so that he can return to his original, undistracted, blissful state of *samādhi.* In the conditioned state, souls are bewildered by innumerable distractions in the name of necessities, sufferings, and enjoyments, and so a devotee prays for the removal of these distractions. The language of devotion may seem extreme to the distracted materialist, but it is actually a prayer for a return to sanity and balance, a return to eternal servitude by the eternal servant of the supreme master.

TEXT 25

मज्जन्मनः फलमिदं मधुकैटभारे
मत्प्रार्थनीयमदनुग्रह एष एव ।
त्वद्भृत्यभृत्यपरिचारकभृत्यभृत्य-
भृत्यस्य भृत्य इति मां स्मर लोकनाथ ॥२५॥

maj-janmanaḥ phalam idaṁ madhu-kaiṭabhāre
mat-prārthanīya-mad-anugraha eṣa eva
tvad-bhṛtya-bhṛtya-paricāraka-bhṛtya-bhṛtya-
bhṛtyasya bhṛtya iti māṁ smara loka-nātha

mat—my; *janmanaḥ*—of the birth; *phalam*—the fruit; *idam*—this; *madhu-kaiṭabha-are*—O enemy of Madhu and Kaiṭabha; *mat*—by me; *prārthanīya*—prayed for; *mat*—to me; *anugrahaḥ*—mercy; *eṣaḥ*—this; *eva*—certainly; *tvat*—Your; *bhṛtya-bhṛtya*—of the servant's servant; *paricāraka*—of the servant; *bhṛtya-bhṛtya-bhṛtyasya*—of the servant of the servant of the servant; *bhṛtyaḥ*—the servant; *iti*—so; *mām*—me; *smara*—think of; *loka*—of the world; *nātha*—O master.

TRANSLATION

O enemy of Madhu and Kaiṭabha, O Lord of the universe, the perfection of my life and the most cherished mercy You could show me would be for You to consider me the servant of the servant of the servant of the servant of the servant of the servant of Your servant.

PURPORT

This verse is startling for its repetition of the word "servant" seven times. One can almost picture all the servants of the Lord whom Kulaśekhara wishes to serve. Direct servants of Lord Kṛṣṇa are Śrīmatī Rādhārāṇī or Lord Balarāma and other *gopīs* and cowherd boys. Some of the *gopīs* and cowherd boys are assistants to the direct servants. Among these assistants are the *mañjarīs,* who help Rādhārāṇī serve Kṛṣṇa and who, according to Her, experience a happiness even greater than Hers. The Vaiṣṇava spiritual masters, especially those in the *mādhurya-rasa,* serve the *gopīs,* and each spiritual master is being served by his disciples. In the modern age Lord Kṛṣṇa appeared as Lord Caitanya, who was served directly by the six Gosvāmīs of Vṛndāvana, and these Gosvāmīs also took disciples, such as Krsnadāsa Kavirāja, who in turn accepted disciples—and His Divine Grace A. C. Bhaktivedanta Swami Prabhupāda is in the eleventh spiritual generation of that Caitanya-sampradāya. So the phrase *tvad-bhṛtya-bhṛtya-paricāraka-bhṛtya-bhṛtya-bhṛtyasya bhṛtyaḥ* is not only pleasing poetry, but it is an accurate description of the *paramparā:* each devotee is serving a previous servant of the Lord.

To consider oneself a servant of all the Vaiṣṇavas and to put their foot-dust on one's head is not demeaning; it is the best way to please the Supreme Personality of Godhead, Lord Kṛṣṇa. Prahlāda Mahārāja told his father that unless one humbly serves the Vaiṣṇavas and "bathes" in the dust of their lotus feet, one can never attain devotional service to Kṛṣṇa.

King Kulaśekhara says that if the Lord grants this prayer it will be the display of His most cherished mercy. But why does he ask to be *so many* times removed from direct service? Why not ask simply to be the servant of the Lord? One reason is that the Supreme Lord does not accept direct service without service to His servants. As Kṛṣṇa states in the *Ādi Purāṇa,*

ye me bhakta-janāḥ pārtha na me bhaktāś ca te janāḥ
mad bhaktānāṁ ca ye bhaktās te me bhaktatamāḥ matāḥ

"My dear Pārtha, those who say they are My devotees are not My devotees, but those who claim to be devotees of My devotees are actually My devotees."

The pure devotee's chief aim is to please his worshipable Lord, and a wise Vaiṣṇava knows what will please Him best—becoming the servant, many times removed, of the Lord's bona fide servants. It is because the servants of God are so dear to the Lord that one can please Him best by pleasing them. Śrīla Prabhupāda compared the process to an ordinary person's attempt to please a very great man. Normally an ordinary man cannot even approach the great man, but if by good fortune he is able to please the great man's pet dog, then he can quickly achieve the favor of the celebrated person.

Another reason a devotee wishes to serve through other devotees is that he is naturally humble. He wants to take that place below, rather than push himself forward. He wants to serve all the devotees, or even worship the place where they have walked. The genuine devotee does not rashly presume that he is a member of the inner circle of the Lord's most dear ones. Lord Caitanya has advised us that if we really wish to chant the holy name constantly, we should consider ourselves "lower that the straw in the street, devoid of all sense of false prestige, and ready to offer all respects to others." We should serve not only recognized devotees but all living entities, by giving them Kṛṣṇa consciousness.

TEXT 26

तत्त्वं ब्रुवाणानि परं परस्तान्
मधु क्षरन्तीव मुदावहानि ।
प्रावर्तय प्राञ्जलिरस्मि जिह्वे
नामानि नारायणगोचराणि ॥२६॥

tattvaṁ bruvāṇāni paraṁ parastān
madhu kṣarantīva mudāvahāni

prāvartaya prāñjalir asmi jihve
nāmāni nārāyaṇa-gocarāṇi

tattvam—the truth; *bruvāṇāni*—which speak; *param*—supreme; *parastāt*—beyond everything superior; *madhu*—honey; *kṣaranti*—dripping; *iva*—as if; *mudā*—joy; *avahāni*—bringing; *prāvartaya*—please recite; *prāñjaliḥ*—with joined palms; *asmi*—I am; *jihve*—O tongue; *nāmāni*—the names; *nārāyaṇa-gocarāṇi*—which refer to Lord Nārāyaṇa.

TRANSLATION

My dear tongue, I stand before you with joined palms and beg you to recite the names of Lord Nārāyaṇa. These names describing the Supreme Absolute Truth bring great pleasure, as if exuding honey.

PURPORT

At first our tongues may be unwilling to chant the Lord's names. Describing the neophyte chanter, Śrīla Bhaktivinoda Ṭhākura states, "Some bear only the burden; others appreciate the true worth of things." Śrīla Rūpa Gosvāmī also recognizes the plight of the beginner and encourages him to pursue his chanting even though it seems dry and unpleasant: "The holy name, character, pastimes, and activities of Kṛṣṇa are all transcendentally sweet like sugar candy. Although the tongue of one afflicted by the jaundice of *avidyā,* ignorance, cannot taste anything sweet, it is wonderful that if a person simply chants these sweet names carefully every day, a natural relish awakens within his tongue, and his disease is gradually destroyed at the root" (*Nectar of Instruction* 7).

We may also take heart in the example of Nāmācārya Haridāsa Ṭhākura. Although born in a Muslim family, he received the mercy of the holy name and began to chant Hare Kṛṣṇa constantly. In this way he achieved the highest perfection of love of Godhead. Indeed, he was such an exalted devotee that Lord Caitanya Himself praised him "as if speaking with five mouths." We cannot imitate Haridāsa Ṭhākura, but it is encouraging to know that although one may be lowborn, one can overcome all obstacles by the mercy of the holy name. Moreover, Haridāsa Ṭhākura always remained very humble and wanted to remain aware of his material disqualifications. He therefore did not want to associate too intimately with Lord Caitanya, and he did not attempt to enter the temple at Jagannātha Purī. Cultivating humility in the mood of Haridāsa Ṭhākura is an absolute requirement for one who wishes to taste the nectar of the holy name and to chant constantly.

The honey within the holy name is remembrance of Kṛṣṇa. That is why chanting the name brings ecstasy. As Śrīla Prabhupāda writes, "The more one chants the names of Kṛṣṇa, the more one becomes attached. Thus service by *śravaṇa* and *kīrtana,* hearing and chanting about Kṛṣṇa, is the beginning. The next process is *smaraṇa*—always remembering Kṛṣṇa. When one is perfect in hearing and chanting, he will always remember Kṛṣṇa. In this third stage he becomes the greatest *yogī*" (*The Matchless Gift,* p. 89). Whether we are still at the beginning stage of *bhakti,* afflicted with *avidyā,* or whether we are starting to appreciate "the true worth of things," let us all go on chanting the holy names of the Lord. And let us relish verses from the authorized devotees who tell us of the honey in the holy name, such as this one by Śrīla Sanātana Gosvāmī:

jayati jayati nāmānanda-rūpaṁ murārer
viramita-nija-dharma-dhyāna-pūjādi-yatnam
katham api sakṛd āttaṁ mukti-daṁ prāṇināṁ yat
paramam amṛtam ekaṁ jīvanaṁ bhūṣaṇaṁ me

"All glories, all glories to the all-blissful holy name of Śrī Kṛṣṇa, which causes the devotee to give up all conventional religious duties, meditation, and worship. When somehow or other uttered even once by a living entity, the holy name awards him liberation. The holy name of Kṛṣṇa is the highest nectar. It is my very life and my only treasure" (*Bṛhad-bhāgavatāmṛta* 1.9).

TEXT 27

नमामि नारायणपादपङ्कजं
करोमि नारायणपूजनं सदा ।
वदामि नारायणनामनिर्मलं
स्मरामि नारायणतत्त्वमव्ययम् ॥२७॥

namāmi nārāyaṇa-pāda-paṅkajaṁ
karomi nārāyaṇa-pūjanaṁ sadā
vadāmi nārāyaṇa-nāma nirmalaṁ
smarāmi nārāyaṇa-tattvam avyayam

namāmi—I offer obeisances; *nārāyaṇa*—of Lord Nārāyaṇa; *pāda-paṅkajam*—to the lotus feet; *karomi*—I do; *nārāyaṇa*—of Lord Nārāyaṇa; *pūjanam*—worship; *sadā*—always; *vadāmi*—I speak; *nārāyaṇa*—of Lord Nārāyaṇa; *nāma*—the name; *nirmalam*—free from contamination; *smarāmi*—I remember; *nārāyaṇa*—of Nārāyaṇa; *tattvam*—truth; *avyayam*—infallible.

TRANSLATION

At every moment I bow down to the lotus feet of Nārāyaṇa, I perform worship to Nārāyaṇa, I recite the pure name of Nārāyaṇa, and I reflect on the infallible truth of Nārāyaṇa.

PURPORT

One may wonder, Is this an exaggeration or perhaps an expression of wishful thinking? The answer is no, this verse describes the practical experience of King Kulaśekhara, a pure devotee. Moreover, such absorption in various services to the Lord is possible not only for King Kulaśekhara but for all sincere devotees. Such twenty-four-hour engagement in the Lord's service is rarely possible at once, but we can take encouragement from Lord Kṛṣṇa's words in the *Bhagavad-gītā* (12.9): "If you cannot fix your mind upon Me without deviation, then follow the regulative principles of *bhakti-yoga.* In this way develop the desire to attain to Me."

King Kulaśekhara first states, *namāmi:* "I offer obeisances." This refers to bowing down to the Lord physically and mentally, thus praying to Him with one's whole being to be placed, as Lord Caitanya said, as "an atom at [His] lotus feet." We offer obeisances because we recognize the inconceivable greatness of the Supreme Lord, and we beg for awareness of our own tinyness and dependence on Him. In addition to following the regulative principles of devotioonal service, we should take time regularly to go beyond the mechanical activity of religious duties, beyond all the relative roles we may play with our family and in our religious institution, and to try to recall that we are actually eternal servants of the Supreme Lord and of all living beings.

The preacher of Kṛṣṇa consciousness should offer mental obeisances to the recipients of his message. Lord Caitanya advised His followers, *yāre dekha tāre kaha kṛṣṇa-upadeśa:* "Impart Kṛṣṇa's teachings to whomever you meet" (Cc. *Madhya* 7.128). By carrying out this order we offer humble obeisances to the Lord within all living entities.

King Kulaśekhara says that he recites the name of Nārāyaṇa at every moment. Śrīla Prabhupāda advised his followers to do the same: "In our Kṛṣṇa consciousness movement we are teaching our followers to chant the Hare Kṛṣṇa *mantra* continuously on beads. Even those who are not accustomed to this practice are advised to chant at least sixteen rounds on beads so they may be trained. . . . *Sadā* means 'always.' Haridāsa Ṭhākura says *nirantara nāma lao:* 'Chant the Hare Kṛṣṇa *mantra* without stopping'" (Cc. *Antya* 3.139, purport).

To chant all the time one has to follow Lord Caitanya's advice—to think oneself lower than the straw in the street and offer all respects to others. In this way one combines reciting the Lord's names and offering obeisances. A person who does not offer respects to God and all God's creatures, who is proud of his material acquisitions, cannot call upon the Lord sincerely. Even if he does occasionally chant the Lord's name, he does so with complacency. A devotee who realizes his actual situation of dependence on Kṛṣṇa calls on the name of the Lord the way a child calls upon his mother. And as stated in previous verses, such a chanter tastes unprecedented nectar in the holy name.

King Kulaśekhara also reflects on the infallible truth of Nārāyaṇa. The conclusion (*siddhānta*) concerning the science of the Supreme Personality of Godhead is received from the scriptures, from the *guru,* and from authorized *sādhus.* One should regularly read and hear the *Śrīmad-Bhagavatam,* the *Bhagavad-gītā,* the *Caitanya-caritāmṛta,* and similar Vaiṣṇava works, and one should also hear realized devotees explain them. One who does so will eventually be able to see all events in a Kṛṣṇa conscious way. This is known as *śāstra-cakṣur,* seeing the world with the vision gained through scriptural knowledge.

And so King Kulaśekhara has offered four activities that should consume all our time without distraction: offering obeisances to the Lord, worshiping Him, chanting His holy names, and thinking of the conclusive truths concerning Him. These practices are included in the ninefold process of devotional service Prahlāda Mahārāja describes in the Seventh Canto of the *Śrīmad-Bhāgavatam* (7.5.23). So whether one performs the activities King Kulaśekhara mentions here or adds the ones Prahlāda Mahārāja recommends—praying, worshiping the Deity, becoming the Lord's friend, and so on—one can move from one activity to another, from one thought to another, and yet stay within the internal, spiritual energy of Lord Nārāyaṇa. Such a fully Kṛṣṇa conscious devotee will transfer at the time of death to the spiritual world, where he will render further services in the blissful company of the Lord and His intimate associates.

TEXTS 28–29

श्रीनाथ नारायण वासुदेव
    श्रीकृष्ण भक्तप्रिय चक्रपाणे ।
श्रीपद्मनाभाच्युत कैटभारे
    श्रीराम पद्माक्ष हरे मुरारे ॥२८॥

अनन्त वैकुण्ठ मुकुन्द कृष्ण
    गोविन्द दामोदर माधवेति ।
वक्तुं समर्थोऽपि न वक्ति कश्चिद्
    अहो जनानां व्यसनाभिमुख्यम् ॥२९॥

śrī-nātha nārāyaṇa vāsudeva
śrī-kṛṣṇa bhakta-priya cakra-pāṇe
śrī-padmanābhācyuta kaiṭabhāre
śrī-rāma padmākṣa hare murāre

ananta vaikuṇṭha mukunda kṛṣṇa
govinda dāmodara mādhaveti
vaktuṁ samartho 'pi na vakti kaścid
aho janānāṁ vyasanābhimukhyam

śrī-nātha—O Lord of the goddess of fortune; *nārāyaṇa*—O resort of all living entities; *vāsudeva*—O supreme proprietor; *śrī-kṛṣṇa*—O Kṛṣṇa, son of Devakī; *bhakta*—toward Your devotees; *priya*—O You who are favorably disposed; *cakra*—the disc weapon; *pāṇe*—O You who hold in Your hand; *śrī*—divine; *padma-nābha*—O You from whose navel grows a lotus; *acyuta*—O infallible Lord; *kaiṭabha-are*—O enemy of Kaiṭabha, *śrī-rāma*—O blessed Rāma; *padma-akṣa*—O lotus-eyed one; *hare*—O remover of misfortune; *mura-are*—O enemy of Mura; *ananta*—O limitless one; *vaikuṇṭha*—O Lord of the spiritual kingdom; *mukunda*—O bestower of liberation; *kṛṣṇa*—O Kṛṣṇa; *govinda*—O master of the cows; *dāmodara*—O You who were tied up as punishment by Your mother; *mādhava*—O Lord of the supreme goddess; *iti*—thus; *vaktum*—to speak; *samarthaḥ*—able; *api*—although; *na vakti*—one does not say; *kaścit*—anything; *aho*—ah; *janānām*—of people; *vyasana*—toward a danger; *ābhimukhyam*—the inclination.

TRANSLATION

O Śrīnātha, Nārāyaṇa, Vāsudeva, divine Kṛṣṇa, O kind friend of Your devotees! O Cakrapāṇi, Padmanābha, Acyuta, Kaiṭabhāri, Rāma, Padmākṣa, Hari, Murāri! O Ananta, Vaikuṇṭha, Mukunda, Kṛṣṇa, Govinda, Dāmodara, Mādhava! Although all people can address You, still they remain silent. Just see how eager they are for their own peril!

PURPORT

The Supreme Personality of Godhead manifests innumerable inconceivable qualities, and to remember and glorify these qualities His devotees address Him by innumerable names. The names themselves are fully invested with the power of the Lord. As Lord Caitanya states in His *Śikṣāṣṭaka* (2), *nāmnām akāri bahudhā nija-sarva-śaktis tatrārpitā niyamitaḥ smaraṇe na kālaḥ:* "O my Lord, O Supreme Personality of Godhead, in Your holy name there is all good fortune for the living entity, and therefore You have many names, such as Kṛṣṇa and Govinda, by which You expand Yourself. You have invested all Your potencies in those names, and there are no hard and fast rules for chanting them."

Śrī Yāmunācārya, who appeared in the same *sampradāya* as King Kulaśekhara, composed a verse lamenting that although the Lord is fully accessible by His many names and qualities, the nondevotees do not approach Him, and thus they bring about their own destruction. In *Bhagavad-gītā* (7.15), Lord Kṛṣṇa summarizes the types of persons who do not surrender to Him:

na māṁ duṣkṛtino mūḍhāḥ prapadyante narādhamāḥ
māyayāpahṛta-jñānā āsuraṁ bhāvam āśritāḥ

"Those miscreants who are grossly foolish, who are the lowest among mankind, whose knowledge is stolen by illusion, and who partake of the atheistic nature of demons do not surrender to Me."

As His Divine Grace Śrīla Prabhupāda traveled worldwide spreading the Kṛṣṇa consciousness movement, he noted that most people could not understand the simplest rudiments of transcendental knowledge. The first lesson of spiritual knowledge is that the self is not the body but rather the soul, and that therefore the soul is the truly important thing. But in Western countries, even among the scholarly elite, people do not understand the nature of the soul, and therefore they fail to understand the real mission of human life—understanding God. One who cannot understand the soul cannot understand God, for the soul is a minute particle of God, and failing to understand the particle, one fails to understand the whole. Instead of even trying to understand the spirit soul, most people ignore it or, even worse, deny its existence entirely. And godless scientists encourage the people in their ignorance by propounding the theory that life arises from matter. Śrīla Prabhupāda decried this atheistic theory and exposed the fact that it could not be proved. Thus he said that civilized countries, especially in the West, were living in a fool's paradise.

King Kulaśekhara notes that we ignore God and His many names and activities at our peril. This peril is not only individual but collective. Materialists try to live in a technological paradise, but the paradise is lost when war breaks out or other calamities strike. Although Śrīla Prabhupāda noted that fools become angry when called fools, he never hesitated to boldly criticize the foolish materialists in his books and lectures. But he didn't simply criticize: he offered the teachings and the example that can bring relief to the whole world. He taught the members of his International Society for Krishna Consciousness to live in a way that leaves ample time for spiritual advancement. The Society is meant to be an example for the whole world, a community whose members have reduced their problems and are simply interested living a God-centered life.

Though the four kinds of unsurrendered persons Kṛṣṇa mentions in the *Bhagavad-gītā* are not interested in surrendering to Him, the devotees continue their efforts, satisfied to set the example their spiritual master has requested and to help conditioned souls wherever possible.

TEXT 30

भक्तापायभुजाङ्गगारुडमणिस्त्रैलोक्यरक्षामणिर्
गोपीलोचनचातकाम्बुदमणिः सौन्दर्यमुद्रामणिः ।
यः कान्तामणिरुक्मिणीघनकुचद्वन्द्वैकभूषामणिः
श्रेयो देवशिखामणिर्दिशतु नो गोपालचूडामणिः ॥३०॥

bhaktāpāya-bhujāṅga-gāruḍa-maṇis trailokya-rakṣā-maṇir
gopī-locana-cātakāmbuda-maṇiḥ saundarya-mudrā-maṇiḥ
yaḥ kāntā-maṇi-rukmiṇī-ghana-kuca-dvandvaika-bhūṣā-maṇiḥ
śreyo deva-śikhā-maṇir diśatu no gopāla-cūḍā-maṇiḥ

bhakta—His devotees; *apāya*—who takes away; *bhuja-aṅga*—whose arms; *gāruḍa*—riding on the great bird Garuḍa; *maṇiḥ*—the jewel; *trai-lokya*—of the three worlds; *rakṣā*—for protection; *maṇiḥ*—the jewel; *gopī*—of the cowherd girls; *locana*—of the eyes; *cātaka*—for the *cātaka* birds; *ambuda*—of clouds; *maṇiḥ*—the jewel; *saundarya*—displaying beauty; *mudrā*—of gestures; *maṇiḥ*—the jewel; *yaḥ*—who; *kāntā*—of consorts; *maṇi*—who is the jewel; *rukmiṇī*—of Rukmiṇī; *ghana*—full; *kuca-dvandva*—of the two breasts; *eka*—the one; *bhūṣā*—decorative; *maṇiḥ*—jewel; *śreyaḥ*—ultimate benefit; *deva*—of the demigods; *śikhā-maṇiḥ*—the crown jewel; *diśatu*—may He grant; *naḥ*—to us; *gopāla*—of cowherds; *cūḍā-maṇiḥ*—the crest jewel.

TRANSLATION

He is the jewel riding on the back of Garuḍa, who carries away the Lord's devotees on his wings. He is the magic jewel protecting the three worlds, the jewellike cloud attracting the *cātaka*-bird eyes of the *gopīs*, and the jewel among all who gesture gracefully. He is the only

jeweled ornament on the ample breasts of Queen Rukmiṇī, who is herself the jewel of beloved consorts. May that crown jewel of all gods, the best of the cowherds, grant us the supreme benediction.

PURPORT

In this verse King Kulaśekhara gives us glimpses of Lord Kṛṣṇa in some of His various *līlās*. In each example, the Lord is described as *maṇi,* a jewel. Like a jewel, He is self-effulgent, very beautiful, and highly valuable.

Without a jewel, a ring-setting looks empty, and so without Kṛṣṇa, Garuḍa would have no extraordinary importance, although he is a large and powerful bird. Without Kṛṣṇa, the *gopīs*' eyes would have no place to rest and nothing to see, just as a *cātaka* bird remains restless until it sees a rain-bearing and life-giving cloud. As Lord Caitanya says in the mood of a *gopī,* "The whole world appears vacant without You." In the absence of Kṛṣṇa, the gods would be without their crest jewel, and their own value would fall away. Thus Lord Kṛṣṇa is the absolutely essential figure in His own *līlā* in the spiritual world, as well as in all the operations of the material worlds. As He states in the *Bhagavad-gītā* (7.7), "Everything rests upon Me, as pearls are strung on a thread."

When a soul misuses his free will, he tries to become the center of existence and thinks he can do without Kṛṣṇa. This mistake is illustrated in the story of Satrājit, who once possessed a wondrous jewel called Syamantaka, which he wore in a locket around his neck. When Satrājit entered Dvārakā, Kṛṣṇa asked him to deliver the jewel to the king, Ugrasena. But instead Satrājit installed the jewel in a temple, worshiped it, and gained 170 pounds of gold daily. Because of his claim that the jewel did not belong to Kṛṣṇa, King Satrājit and his family suffered in many ways. The king found peace only when he realized that the Syamantaka should be given to the supreme jewel, Lord Kṛṣṇa. And so he gave both the jewel and his daughter, Satyabhāmā, to the Lord.

TEXT 31

शत्रुच्छेदैकमन्त्रं सकलमुपनिषद्वाक्यसम्पूजयमन्त्रं
संसारोच्छेदमन्त्रं समुचिततमसः सङ्घनिर्याणमन्त्रम् ।

सर्वैश्वर्यैकमन्त्रं व्यसनभुजगसन्दष्टसन्त्राणमन्त्रं
जिह्वे श्रीकृष्णमन्त्रं जप जप सततं जन्मसाफल्यमन्त्रम् ॥३१॥

śatru-cchedaika-mantraṁ sakalam upaniṣad-vākya-sampūjya-mantraṁ
saṁsāroccheda-mantraṁ samucita-tamasaḥ saṅgha-niryāṇa-mantram
sarvaiśvaryaika-mantraṁ vyasana-bhujaga-sandaṣṭa-santrāṇa-mantraṁ
jihve śrī-kṛṣṇa-mantraṁ japa japa satataṁ janma-sāphalya-mantram

śatru—enemies; *cheda*—for destroying; *eka*—the only; *mantram*—mystic chant; *sakalam*—entire; *upaniṣat*—of the *Upaniṣads; vākya*—by the words; *sampūjya*—worshiped; *mantram*—the mystic chant; *saṁsāra*—the cycle of birth and death; *uccheda*—which uproots; *mantram*—the mystic chant; *samucita*—accumulated; *tamasaḥ*—of darkness; *saṅgha*—the mass; *niryāṇa*—for driving away; *mantram*—the mystic chant; *sarva*—all; *aiśvarya*—for opulence; *eka*—the only; *mantram*—mystic chant; *vyasana*—of material distress; *bhujaga*—by the snake; *sandaṣṭa*—for those who have been bitten; *santrāṇa*—saving; *mantram*—the mystic chant; *jihve*—O my tongue; *śrī-kṛṣṇa*—of Śrī Kṛṣṇa; *mantram*—the mystic chant; *japa japa*—please repeatedly chant; *satatam*—always; *janma*—of one's birth; *sāphalya*—for the success; *mantram*—the mystic chant.

TRANSLATION

O tongue, please constantly chant the *mantra* composed of Śrī Kṛṣṇa's names. This is the only *mantra* for destroying all enemies, the *mantra* worshiped by every word of the *Upaniṣads,* the *mantra* that uproots *saṁsāra,* the *mantra* that drives away all the darkness of ignorance, the *mantra* for attaining infinite opulence, the *mantra* for curing those bitten by the poisonous snake of worldly distress, and the *mantra* for making one's birth in this world successful.

PURPORT

A *mantra* is a sound vibration that delivers the mind from illusion. When a person chants a *mantra* consisting of the Lord's names, his mind is freed of distress and he comes to the state of transcendental peace in God consciousness. Of all such *mantras,* however, the one

King Kulaśekhara recommends is a *kṛṣṇa-mantra*—in other words, one composed of Kṛṣṇa's names. One of these is the Hare Kṛṣṇa *mahā-mantra,* which Lord Caitanya chanted and which the *Upaniṣads* proclaim the best *mantra* for Kali-yuga:

hare kṛṣṇa hare kṛṣṇa kṛṣṇa kṛṣṇa hare hare
hare rāma hare rāma rāma rāma hare hare

iti ṣoḍaśakaṁ nāmnāṁ kali-kalmaṣa-nāśanam
nātaḥ parataropāyaḥ sarva-vedeṣu dṛśyate

"Hare Kṛṣṇa, Hare Kṛṣṇa, Kṛṣṇa Kṛṣṇa, Hare Hare/ Hare Rāma, Hare Rāma, Rāma Rāma, Hare Hare. These sixteen names composed of thirty-two syllables are the only means of counteracting the evil effects of the Kali-yuga. After searching through all the Vedic literature, one cannot find a method of religion for this age so sublime as the chanting of the Hare Kṛṣṇa *mantra*" (*Kali-santaraṇa Upaniṣad*).

King Kulaśekhara declares that the *kṛṣṇa-mantra* destroys one's enemies. We find one confirmation of this in the story of Ajāmila, who chanted the name Nārāyaṇa and was protected from the agents of death. Elsewhere the *Śrīmad-Bhāgavatam* states,

āpannaḥ saṁsṛtiṁ ghorāṁ yan-nāma vivaśo gṛṇan
tataḥ sadyo vimucyeta yad bibheti svayaṁ bhayam

"Living beings who are entangled in the complicated meshes of birth and death can be freed immediately by even unconsciously chanting the holy name of Kṛṣṇa, which is feared by fear personified" (*Bhāg.* 1.1.14). Also, chanting the holy name of Kṛṣṇa destroys the six mental enemies: lust, anger, greed, illusion, madness, and envy.

Next Kulaśekhara says that the *kṛṣṇa-mantra* is worshiped throughout the *Upaniṣads.* For the most part, the *Upaniṣads* describe the personal form of the Lord indirectly, yet they always point toward Kṛṣṇa. Śrīla Rūpa Gosvāmī reveals this inner meaning of the *Upaniṣads* in his *Nāmāṣṭaka* (1):

nikhila-śruti-mauli-ratna-māla-
dyuti-nīrājita-pāda-paṅkajānta

ayi mukta-kulair upāsyamānāṁ
paritas tvāṁ hari-nāma saṁśrayāmi

"O Hari-nāma! The tips of the toes of Your lotus feet are constantly being worshiped by the glowing radiance emanating from the string of gems known as the *Upaniṣads,* the crown jewels of all the *Vedas.* You are eternally adored by liberated souls such as Nārada and Śukadeva. O Hari-nāma! I take complete shelter of You."

The *kṛṣṇa-mantra* also uproots *saṁsāra.* Lord Caitanya confirms this in His *Śikṣāṣṭaka* (1), where He states, *bhava-mahā-dāvāgni-nirvāpanam:* "The congregational chanting of the Hare Kṛṣṇa *mantra* extinguishes the blazing fire of repeated birth and death." The *kṛṣṇa-mantra* is also most effective for driving away the darkness of ignorance. As Lord Caitanya says in the same verse, *vidyā-vadhū-jīvanam:* "Chanting Hare Kṛṣṇa is the life and soul of transcendental knowledge." Also, the second verse of the *Caitanya-caritāmṛta* compares Lord Caitanya and Lord Nityānanda, the foremost propagators of the chanting of Kṛṣṇa's names, to the sun and moon: "They have arisen simultaneously on the horizon of Gauḍa [Bengal] to dissipate the darkness of ignorance and thus wonderfully bestow benediction upon all." Elaborating on this point, Śrīla Kṛṣṇadāsa Kavirāja informs us that the material sun and moon are able to dissipate the darkness of the external world, "but these two brothers [Lord Caitanya and Lord Nityānanda] dissipate the darkness of the inner core of the heart and thus help one to meet the two kinds of *bhāgavatas* [persons or things related to the Supreme Personality of Godhead]" (Cc. *Ādi* 1.98).

King Kulaśekhara glorifies the *kṛṣṇa-mantra* as the bestower of infinite opulence. The most valuable thing, even more valuable than the *cintāmaṇi* stone of this world, is love of Godhead. "Simply chanting the Hare Kṛṣṇa *mahā-mantra* without offenses vanquishes all sinful activity. Thus pure devotional service, which is the cause of love of Godhead, becomes manifest" (Cc. *Ādi* 8.26).

King Kulaśekhara also praises the *kṛṣṇa-mantra* as a type of medicine that relieves the suffering of those who have been bitten by the snake of material distress. In Śrīla Bhaktivinoda Ṭhākura's song *Aruṇodaya-kīrtana,* Lord Caitanya says to the people of the world, "I have brought the medicine for destroying the illusion of Māyā. Now pray for this *hari-nāma mahā-mantra* and take it."

TEXT 32

व्यामोहप्रशमौषधं मुनिमनोवृत्तिप्रवृत्त्यौषधं
दैत्येन्द्रार्तिकरौषधं त्रिभुवने सञ्जीवनैकौषधम् ।
भक्तात्यन्तहितौषधं भवभयप्रध्वंसनैकौषधं
श्रेयःप्राप्तिकरौषधं पिब मनः श्रीकृष्णदिव्यौषधम् ॥३२॥

vyāmoha-praśamauṣadhaṁ muni-mano-vṛtti-pravṛtty-auṣadhaṁ
daityendrārti-karauṣadhaṁ tri-bhuvane sañjīvanaikauṣadham
bhaktātyanta-hitauṣadhaṁ bhava-bhaya-pradhvaṁsanaikauṣadhaṁ
śreyaḥ-prāpti-karauṣadhaṁ piba manaḥ śrī-kṛṣṇa-divyauṣadham

vyāmoha—utter bewilderment; *praśama*—for subduing; *auṣadham*—the herbal medicine; *muni*—of sages; *manaḥ*—of the minds; *vṛtti*—the functioning; *pravṛtti*—which initiates; *auṣadham*—the medicine; *daitya*—of the demoniac descendants of Diti; *indra*—for the leaders; *ārti*—distress; *kara*—which causes; *auṣadham*—the medicine; *tri-bhuvane*—within the three worlds; *sañjīvana*—for bringing the dead back to life; *eka*—the only; *auṣadham*—medicine; *bhakta*—of the Lord's devotees; *atyanta*—absolute; *hita*—for benefit; *auṣadham*—the medicine; *bhava*—of material existence; *bhaya*—fear; *pradhvaṁsana*—for destroying; *eka*—the only; *auṣadham*—medicine; *śreyaḥ*—of supreme good; *prāpti*—attainment; *kara*—which effects; *auṣadham*—the medicine; *piba*—just drink; *manaḥ*—O mind; *śrī-kṛṣṇa*—of Lord Śrī Kṛṣṇa; *divya*—transcendental; *auṣadham*—the medicinal herb.

TRANSLATION

O mind, please drink the transcendental medicine of Śrī Kṛṣṇa's glories. It is the perfect medicine for curing the disease of bewilderment, for inspiring sages to engage their minds in meditation, and for tormenting the mighty Daitya demons. It alone is the medicine for restoring the three worlds to life and for bestowing unlimited blessings on the Supreme Lord's devotees. Indeed, it is the only medicine that can destroy one's fear of material existence and lead one to the attainment of the supreme good.

PURPORT

My colleague Gopīparāṇadhana Prabhu notes, "*Maṇi, mantra,* and *auṣadha* [jewels, *mantras,* and medicine] are often grouped together by Vedic philosophers as examples of things in this world that have *acintya-śakti* (inconceivable energy)." Since the Supreme Personality of Godhead and His energies are inconceivable, it is understandable why the poets and philosophers compare Him to jewels and medicine and praise the wonderful powers of *mantras* composed of His names.

Aside from jewels, *mantras,* and medicine, every living being in the creation possesses *acintya-śakti* to some degree. Although human beings often consider themselves the most powerful of all God's creatures, many lowly creatures possess abilities far beyond those of human beings. For example, growing grass endures trampling and stays out all night in freezing weather without a protest. A human being is not so tolerant. Frogs possess an inconceivable ability to maintain their lives even while buried under the earth. Hummingbirds and insects are flying machines so sophisticated that they can outmaneuver airplanes in many ways. Although scientists tend to think of their work as demystifying the secrets of the universe, they admit that nature at its most basic level remains inconceivable.

The presence of *acintya-śakti* in both the smallest and the greatest aspects of the universe should lead us to ask, Who is the source of this inconceivable energy? That source is described in the *Brahma-saṁhitā* as the *acintya-rūpa,* or inconceivable form, of Lord Govinda, the Supreme Personality of Godhead.

The process of *bhakti-yoga* is also inconceivable. Every person fortunate enough to take up the process of Kṛṣṇa consciousness can attest to the inconceivable potency of the medicine of devotional service. Although we may have tried to give up vices before encountering Kṛṣṇa consciousness, we could not do so for long. But as soon as we began serving Kṛṣṇa and the pure devotee and chanting the Lord's holy names, the "impossible" was easily accomplished. The inconceivable energy that brings about these changes is called *kṛṣṇa-śakti.*

By the grace of the Supreme Lord, a pure devotee possesses this *kṛṣṇa-śakti,* and when he chants the holy name or speaks about Kṛṣṇa, the potent sound enters the consciousness of the receptive hearer and purifies him. By contrast, when a nondevotee speaks of Kṛṣṇa or chants His name, the effect on the hearer is not purifiying but poisonous. Only one who is directly empowered by the Supreme Lord can spread Kṛṣṇa consciousness through *kṛṣṇa-śakti.* Thus only from the pure devotees can we gain the jewel, *mantra,* or medicine of devotional service, from which we can derive the inconceivable benefits of love of God.

TEXT 33

कृष्ण त्वदीयपदपङ्कजपञ्जरान्तम्
अद्यैव मे विशतु मानसराजहंसः ।
प्राणप्रयाणसमये कफवातपित्तैः
कण्ठावरोधनविधौ स्मरणं कुतस्ते ॥३३॥

kṛṣṇa tvadīya-pada-paṅkaja-pañjarāntam
adyaiva me viśatu mānasa-rāja-haṁsaḥ
prāṇa-prayāṇa-samaye kapha-vāta-pittaiḥ
kaṇṭhāvarodhana-vidhau smaraṇaṁ kutas te

kṛṣṇa—O Lord Kṛṣṇa; *tvadīya*—Your; *pada*—feet; *paṅkaja*—lotus flower; *pañjara*—the network; *antam*—the edge; *adya*—now, at this moment; *eva*—certainly; *me*—my; *viśatu*—may enter; *mānasa*—mind; *rāja*—royal; *haṁsa*—swan; *prāṇa-prayāṇa*—of death; *samaye*—at the time; *kapha*—mucus; *vāta*—air; *pittaiḥ*—and with bile; *kaṇṭha*—throat; *avarodhana-vidhau*—when it is choked; *smaraṇam*—remembrance; *kutaḥ*—how is it possible; *te*—of You.

TRANSLATION

O Lord Kṛṣṇa, at this moment let the royal swan of my mind enter the tangled stems of the lotus of Your feet. How will it be possible for me to remember You at the time of death, when my throat will be choked up with mucus, bile, and air?

PURPORT

Of all the verses of the *Mukunda-mālā-stotra,* this one was the most beloved of Śrīla Prabhupāda. He frequently quoted it and sang it as a *bhajana.* On one of the first record albums His Divine Grace produced, he sang this *śloka* as a complete song. Devotees who served Śrīla Prabhupāda often heard him sing it as he went about his daily activities, or sometimes alone in his room. He also quoted it many times in his purports. Here he explains it in the purport to the second verse of the Eighth Chapter of his *Bhagavad-gītā As It Is,* in reference to the word *prayāṇa-kāla,* which carries the same meaning as *prāṇa-prayāṇa-samaye* in Kulaśekhara's verse:

> Now, the word *prayāṇa-kāle* in this [*Bhagavad-gītā*] verse is very significant because whatever we do in life will be tested at the time of death. Arjuna is very anxious to know of those who are constantly engaged in Kṛṣṇa consciousness. What should be their position at that final moment? At the time of death all the bodily functions are disrupted, and the mind is not in a proper condition. Thus disturbed by the bodily situation, one may not be able to remember the Supreme Lord. Mahārāja Kulaśekhara, a great devotee, prays, "My dear Lord, just now I am quite healthy, and it is better that I die immediately so that the swan of my mind can seek entrance at the stem of Your lotus feet." The metaphor is used because the swan, a bird of the water, takes pleasure in digging into the lotus flowers; its sporting proclivity is to enter the lotus flower. Mahārāja Kulaśekhara says to the Lord, "Now my mind is undisturbed, and I am quite healthy. If I die immediately, thinking of Your lotus feet, then I am sure that my performance of Your devotional service will become perfect. But if I have to wait for my natural death, then I do not know what will happen, because at that time the bodily functions will be disrupted, my throat will be choked up, and I do not know whether I shall be able to chant Your name. Better let me die immediately."

Later in the Eighth Chapter Lord Kṛṣṇa says that the exact moment of death is crucial: "Whatever state of being one remembers when he quits his body, . . . that state he will attain without fail" (Bg. 8.6). And in his purports Śrīla Prabhupāda repeatedly recommends chanting the Hare Kṛṣṇa *mantra* as the best process for remembering Kṛṣṇa at the time of death and successfully transferring oneself to the spiritual world.

The practical difficulty, brought up in Kulaśekhara's verse, is that although it is crucial to remember Kṛṣṇa at the time of death, that time also produces the greatest disruption of one's physical and mental functions. Śrīla Prabhupāda explained that death occurs when the body becomes so painful that the soul finds it unbearable to live in the body any longer. Therefore the paradox: At the time when we should be the most meditative, fixing our mind on Kṛṣṇa and preparing to transfer ourselves to the spiritual world, we are also faced with the greatest possible distraction in the form of agonizing pain. Thus here King Kulaśekhara prays to die now, in good health, so he will be able to absorb his mind in thoughts of Kṛṣṇa's lotus feet.

The *ācāryas* have assured us that the essence of Kṛṣṇa consciousness is our lifelong devotional activities and sentiments. Kṛṣṇa will not disqualify or discount our accumulated devotional activities due to a last moment epileptic fit or sudden heart failure. Nevertheless, we should always practice chanting Hare Kṛṣṇa so that we will be able to "pass the test" at the end.

In the *Īśopaniṣad* (17), a devotee requests the Lord: "[At the moment of my death,] please remember all that I have done for You." In his purport Śrīla Prabhupāda informs us that Kṛṣṇa does not have to be reminded; He is the witness within our heart, and He also desires—more than we do—that we come back to Him, back to Godhead. Considering the trauma of death and the dangerous quirks of fate, however, Mahārāja Kulaśekhara prays that he may die immediately rather than wait for old age, when he may forget Kṛṣṇa in the agony of his death throes.

TEXT 34

चेतश्चिन्तय कीर्तयस्व रसने नम्रीभव त्वं शिरो
हस्तावञ्जलिसम्पुटं रचयतं वन्दस्व दीर्घं वपुः ।
आत्मन्संश्रय पुण्डरीकनयनं नागाचलेन्द्रस्थितं
धन्यं पुण्यतमं तदेव परमं दैवं हि सत्सिद्धये ॥३४॥

cetaś cintaya kīrtayasva rasane namrī-bhava tvaṁ śiro
hastāv añjali-sampuṭaṁ racayataṁ vandasva dīrghaṁ vapuḥ
ātman saṁśraya puṇḍarīka-nayanaṁ nāgācalendra-sthitaṁ
dhanyaṁ puṇya-tamaṁ tad eva paramaṁ daivaṁ hi sat-siddhaye

cetaḥ—O mind; *cintaya*—please think; *kīrtayasva*—please glorify; *rasane*—O tongue; *namrī*—bowed down; *bhava*—become; *tvam*—you;

śiraḥ—O head; *hastau*—O hands; *añjali-sampuṭam*—palms folded in supplication; *racayatam*—please make; *vandasva*—please offer obeisances; *dīrgham*—outstretched; *vapuḥ*—O body; *ātman*—O heart; *saṁśraya*—take full shelter; *puṇḍarīka*—like lotuses; *nayanam*—of Him whose eyes; *nāga*—on the serpent; *acala*—of mountains; *indra*—like the king; *sthitam*—seated; *dhanyam*—all-auspicious; *puṇya-tamam*—supremely purifying; *tat*—He; *eva*—alone; *paramam*—the topmost; *daivam*—Deity; *hi*—indeed; *sat*—of permanent perfection; *siddhaye*—for the achievement.

TRANSLATION

O mind, think of the lotus-eyed Lord who reclines on the mountainlike serpent Ananta. O tongue, glorify Him. O head, bow down to Him. O hands, join your palms in supplication to Him. O body, offer outstretched obeisances to Him. O heart, take full shelter of Him. That Supreme Lord is the topmost Deity. It is He alone who is all-auspicious and supremely purifying, He alone who awards eternal perfection.

PURPORT

This verse is similar to Text 20, wherein the poet instructs his mind, his tongue, his head, and other parts of his body to serve the Lord with full, reverent devotion. Here King Kulaśekhara also offers us some succinct reasons *why* the Lord is worshipable. He is no mortal being but rather the inconceivable Mahā-Viṣṇu, who lies on the serpent couch Ananta Śeṣa. Lord Śeṣa is Himself the resting place of all the universes, and Mahā-Viṣṇu is the omnipotent source of all creation.

The Supreme Absolute Truth is complete along with His personal energies, who serve and worship Him. Just as a king is complete only when he interacts with his loving subjects, so the Parabrahman is complete along with his worshipers. And the devotees are fully satisfied only when rendering devotional service to the Lord. Throughout his prayers, King Kulaśekhara advocates the relationship of the eternal servant with his eternal Lord. He never suggests that the living entities can become one in all respects with the Supreme, or that both the servants and the Lord will ultimately lose their identity in impersonal Brahman. The impersonal theory of the Absolute is an interpretive one, and does not come directly from the Vedic scriptures. The *Vedas* personified make this statement in the *Śrīmad-Bhāgavatam* (10.87.30):

aparimitā dhruvās tanu-bhṛto yadi sarva-gatās
tarhi na śāsyateti niyamo dhruva netarathā
ajani ca yan-mayaṁ tad avimucya niyantṛ bhavet
samam anujānatāṁ yad amataṁ mata-duṣṭatayā

"O supreme eternal! If the embodied living entities were eternal and all-pervading like You, then they would not be under Your control. But if the living entities are accepted as minute energies of Your Lordship, then they are at once subject to Your supreme control. Therefore real liberation entails surrender by the living entities to Your control, and that surrender will make them happy. In that constitutional position only can they be controllers. Therefore, men with limited knowledge who advocate the monistic theory that God and the living entities are equal in all respects are actually misleading themselves and others."

Worship of the Supreme Lord is auspicious and purifying. It clears all dirt from our heart, including the illusion that we are the prime mover in our world and the center of enjoyment. To worship someone or something greater than ourselves is natural, but we often mistake a great person or demigod as the proper object of worship. In the *Bhagavad-gītā* Lord Kṛṣṇa makes it clear that He alone is the only proper object of worship. And in this verse King Kulaśekhara reiterates this point by stating that the lotus-eyed Supreme Lord is the topmost Deity. For universal management Lord Kṛṣṇa expands into many Viṣṇu forms and empowers millions of demigods. Thus there are innumerable deities, or *īśvaras* (controllers), but the Supreme Personality of Godhead is the topmost controller of all.

King Kulaśekhara's prayer calls to mind similar prayers in the *Śrīmad-Bhāgavatam* and other Vedic *śāstras,* uttered by devotees who attained the direct vision (*darśana*) of the Supreme Personality of Godhead. The pure devotees always receive the *darśana* of the Lord in a mood of worshipful ecstasy. They never consider Him an ordinary human being of this universe; nor do they seek to lose their identities and merge into His impersonal effulgence. The devotional sentiments such exalted Vaiṣṇavas express evince the natural awakening of the soul as it comes into the presence of the Lord. The soul becomes humbled and purified and worships his beloved Lord with eloquent prayers and praises. In reciprocation, the Lord bestows His mercy upon His devotees.

In this prayer King Kulaśekhara speaks of the *ṣaṭ-siddhi,* or permanent achievement, awarded by the Supreme Lord. This refers to the personal liberation of going back to Godhead. The *jīvas* are qualitatively one with Kṛṣṇa, and when they come together with Him, a natural attraction occurs. The devotee then wants to use all his faculties to worship the Supreme Lord, who is auspicious to worship and inconceivably great. As great as He is, however, He doesn't force reciprocation. Kṛṣṇa makes this clear in the *Bhagavad-gītā* (4.11): "As they approach Me, I reciprocate with them." Thus it is up to the devotee to choose to serve the Lord out of his own free will.

This verse is, therefore, a call to one's free will. It is a prayer to one's own self to not misuse one's God-given faculties but to engage them in the Lord's service and worship. Because Kṛṣṇa is supremely independent and we are part and parcel of Him, we have minute free will, and so the all-important decision is in our own hands. As Prabhupāda would say, "Man is the architect of his own fortune." Hearing the prayers of King Kulaśekhara inspires us to use our free will properly.

TEXT 35

शृण्वञ्जनार्दनकथागुणकीर्तनानि
देहे न यस्य पुलकोद्गमरोमराजिः ।
नोत्पद्यते नयनयोर्विमलाम्बुमाला
धिक् तस्य जीवितमहो पुरुषाधमस्य ॥३५॥

śṛṇvañ janārdana-kathā-guṇa-kīrtanāni
dehe na yasya pulakodgama-roma-rājiḥ
notpadyate nayanayor vimalāmbu-mālā
dhik tasya jīvitam aho puruṣādhamasya

śṛṇvan—hearing; *janārdana*—of Lord Janārdana; *kathā*—histories; *guṇa*—of His qualities; *kīrtanāni*—and glorification; *dehe*—in the body;

na—not; *yasya*—of whom; *pulaka-udgama*—bristling; *roma*—of hair on the limbs; *rājiḥ*—in rows; *na utpadyate*—there does not arise; *nayanayoḥ*—in the eyes; *vimala*—pure; *amba*—of water; *mālā*—a continuous flow; *dhik*—condemnation; *tasya*—of him; *jīvitam*—on the life; *aho*—ah; *puruṣa*—of such a person; *adhamasya*—most degraded.

TRANSLATION

One who hears descriptions of Lord Janārdana's pastimes and glorious qualities but whose bodily hair fails to bristle in ecstasy and whose eyes fail to flood with tears of pure love—such a person is indeed the most degraded rascal. What a condemned life he leads!

PURPORT

Hearing authorized descriptions of the Supreme Lord from the Vedic literature should produce ecstasy. This is the symptom of genuine Kṛṣṇa consciousness. Kṛṣṇa consciousness is not a subject to be studied as mythology or as comparative religion, and certainly not as a means of reaching impersonal meditation. Merely to be neutral concerning God or to theoretically acknowledge, "Yes, I believe God exists," is not enough. Hearing about Lord Kṛṣṇa should initially produce a regret within the conditioned soul that he has been so long separated from his master, protector, and best friend. Ultimately, with tears of love, he should feel pure affection with the revival of his natural and all-fulfilling relationship with the Lord.

The process of *bhakti* has three stages: *sambandha, abhidheya,* and *prayojana.* In the first stage one hears from authorized sources and awakens to the understanding of the Supreme Personality of Godhead, oneself, the creation, and the relationship among all these. One then realizes the supreme value of *bhakti-yoga,* devotional service unto the all-attractive Lord. In the second stage, called *abhidheya,* one engages in the practical activities of devotional service. This culminates in the final stage, *prayojana,* in which one achieves pure love of God, the goal of life.

In a *Śrīmad-Bhāgavatam* verse similar to this one by King Kulaśekhara, Śukadeva Gosvāmī describes the unfortunate position of one who doesn't awaken to the message of Godhead:

tad aśma-sāraṁ hṛdayaṁ batedaṁ
yad gṛhyamāṇair hari-nāma-dheyaiḥ
na vikriyetātha yadā vikāro
netre jalaṁ gātra-ruheṣu harṣaḥ

"Certainly that heart is steel-framed which, in spite of one's chanting the holy name of the Lord with concentration, does not change and feel ecstasy, at which time tears fill the eyes and the hairs stand on end" (*Bhāg.* 2.3.24).

The *ācāryas* warn us that pretenders imitate these symptoms, complete with tears and bristling hair. Therefore the most reliable symptoms of advancement are detachment from material pleasures and steady, sincere service to the Lord under the guidance of the spiritual master.

This does not negate, however, the importance of ecstasy. In His *Śikṣāṣṭaka* (2) Lord Caitanya, taking the role of a conditioned soul, laments that although He chants the holy name, He fails to achieve ecstasy because He is so unfortunate that He cannot stop committing offenses. Thus if we want to progress toward love of Godhead, we must study and carefully avoid the ten offenses to the holy name. (See *The Nectar of Devotion*, p. 72.)

One who is fortunate enough to get the association of a pure devotee of the Lord can rectify all these bad habits. Otherwise, one will remain steel-hearted and unfit to advance in devotional service. Śrīla Prabhupāda writes, "A complete progressive march on the return path home, back to Godhead, will depend on the instruction of the revealed scriptures directed by realized devotees." By serving the pure devotee one will automatically experience the progressive and ecstatic stages of *bhakti*, without disappointment or imitation.

TEXT 36

अन्धस्य मे हृतविवेकमहाधनस्य
चौरैः प्रभो बलिभिरिन्द्रियनामधेयैः ।
मोहान्धकूपकुहरे विनिपातितस्य
देवेश देहि कृपणस्य करावलम्बम् ॥३६॥

andhasya me hṛta-viveka-mahā-dhanasya
cauraiḥ prabho balibhir indriya-nāmadheyaiḥ
mohāndha-kūpa-kuhare vinipātitasya
deveśa dehi kṛpaṇasya karāvalambam

andhasya—who is blind; *me*—of me; *hṛta*—stolen; *viveka*—discrimination; *mahā*—great; *dhanasya*—whose wealth; *cauraiḥ*—by thieves; *prabho*—O master; *balibhiḥ*—powerful; *indriya*—as the senses; *nāmadheyaiḥ*—who are named; *moha*—of delusion; *andha-kūpa*—of the pitch-dark well; *kuhare*—into the cavity; *vinipātitasya*—thrown down; *deva*—of the demigods; *īśa*—O supreme controller; *dehi*—give; *kṛpaṇasya*—to this unfortunate person; *kara*—of the hand; *avalambam*—the aid.

TRANSLATION

O Lord, the powerful thieves of my senses have blinded me by stealing my most precious possession, my discrimination, and they have thrown me deep into the pitch-dark well of delusion. Please, O Lord of lords, extend Your hand and save this wretched soul.

PURPORT

In texts 20, 26, 31, and 34, King Kulaśekhara instructed his senses to serve the Lord. But now those same senses have apparently dragged him down into the well of delusion. Of course, the king is a liberated, pure devotee of the Lord, and he is simply taking the role of a fallen conditioned soul for our instruction. But still, one might question why Kulaśekhara has first encouraged us with descriptions of proper sensory engagement in the Lord's service—and then discouraged us with this dreary picture of uncontrolled senses casting the hapless soul into the well of delusion.

The answer is that King Kulaśekhara is simply giving us a realistic picture of the alternatives faced by the living being in the clutches of the material energy. We need a sober view of Māyā's powers if we hope to extricate ourselves. As the *Īśopaniṣad* (11) states,

vidyāṁ cāvidyāṁ ca yas tad vedobhayaṁ saha
avidyayā mṛtyuṁ tīrtvā vidyayāmṛtam aśnute

"Only one who can learn the process of nescience and that of transcendental knowledge side by side can transcend the influence of repeated birth and death and enjoy the full blessings of immortality." The right choice for human beings is *vidyā,* or transcendental knowledge, with restricted sense enjoyment. We are taught about *avidyā* so that we will be fully aware of its dire consequences. Then we can strongly reject it and engage our mind and senses wholeheartedly in devotional service to Kṛṣṇa. As Lord Kṛṣṇa states in the *Bhagavad-gītā* (6.5), "A man must elevate himself by his own mind, not degrade himself. The mind is the friend of the conditioned soul, and his enemy as well."

How to use all of one's faculties in Kṛṣṇa's service was exemplified by Mahārāja Ambarīṣa, who engaged his mind in meditating on the Lord's lotus feet, his words in glorifying the Lord's transcendental qualities, his hands in cleaning the Lord's temple, his ears in hearing the Lord's pastimes, his eyes in seeing the Lord's transcendental forms, his body in touching the bodies of the Lord's devotees, his sense of smell in smelling the flowers offered to the Deity, his tongue in tasting the *tulasī* leaves offered to the Lord, his legs in going to the holy places where the Lord's temples are situated, his head in offering humble obeisances to the Lord, and his desires in fulfilling the Lord's desires.

If despite warnings we follow the wanton dictates of our senses, those senses will lead us into the ditch of deep illusion, just as an unreined horse might drag a chariot into a ditch. If this happens—if we fall deep into sinful life—then our only recourse is to call sincerely upon the Supreme Lord to extricate us. King Kulaśekhara's metaphor is not imaginary, for in India a person will sometimes accidentally fall into a dry, overgrown well known as an *andha-kūpa,* or "blind well." Once at the bottom of the well—if he survives the fall—he cannot possibly get out by himself.

Similarly, we cannot extricate ourselves from the deep well of material life unless we grab the rope of mercy lowered by Kṛṣṇa or His representative. As Śrīla Rūpa Gosvāmī prays in his *Stava-mālā:*

manasija-phaṇi-juṣṭe labdha-pāto 'smi duṣṭe
timira-gahana-rūpe hanta saṁsāra-kūpe
ajita nikhila-rakṣā-hetum uddhāra-dakṣāṁ
upanaya mama haste bhakti-rajjuṁ namas te

"Alas, I have fallen into the deep, dark, filthy well of *saṁsāra,* in which the viper of sex desire dwells. O invincible Lord, the rope of devotional service is the cause of universal protection and is expert at delivering the fallen souls. Please place that rope in my hand. I offer my respectful obeisances unto You."

In a similar mood, Śrīla Raghunātha dāsa Gosvāmī says the following in the fifth verse of his *Manaḥ-śikṣā* ("Instructions to the Mind"):

asac-ceṣṭā-kaṣṭa-prada-vikaṭa-pāśālibhir iha
prakāmaṁ kāmādi-prakaṭa-pathapāti-vyatikaraiḥ
gale baddhvā hanye 'ham iti baka-bhid vartmapa-gaṇe
kuru tvaṁ phut-kārān avati sa yathā tvaṁ mana itaḥ

"The highwaymen of lust and his accomplices—greed, etc.—have waylaid me and bound my neck with the horrible ropes of sinful activities. O mind, please scream out for help, crying 'O Kṛṣṇa! O killer of Baka, I am on the verge of death!' If you do this, then Kṛṣṇa will certainly save me."

To be aware of danger is itself a blessing. If we see the disaster of death and rebirth approaching, we will naturally call out to Kṛṣṇa for help. But if we remain in ignorance we will foolishly continue trying to enjoy sense pleasure, not recognizing that sense gratification implicates us in repeated birth and death. However, once we begin sincerely calling on Kṛṣṇa, in full awareness that we are in mortal danger and that He is our only protector, we are already saved.

TEXT 37

इदं शरीरं परिणामपेशलं
पतत्यवश्यं शतसन्धिजर्जरम् ।
किमौषधं पृच्छसि मूढ दुर्मते
निरामयं कृष्णरसायनं पिब ॥३७॥

idaṁ śarīraṁ pariṇāma-peśalaṁ
pataty avaśyaṁ śata-sandhi-jarjaram
kim auṣadhaṁ pṛcchasi mūḍha durmate
nirāmayaṁ kṛṣṇa-rasāyanaṁ piba

idam—this; *śarīram*—body; *pariṇāma*—as subject to transformation; *peśalam*—attractive; *patati*—falls down; *avaśyam*—inevitably; *śata*—hundreds; *sandhi*—joints; *jarjaram*—having become decrepit; *kim*—why; *auṣadham*—for medication; *pṛcchasi*—you are asking; *mūḍha*—deluded; *durmate*—O fool; *nirāmayam*—prophylactic; *kṛṣṇa*—of Kṛṣṇa; *rasa-ayanam*—the elixir; *piba*—just drink.

TRANSLATION

This body's beauty is fleeting, and at last the body must succumb to death after its hundreds of joints have stiffened with old age. So why, bewildered fool, are you asking for medication? Just take the Kṛṣṇa elixir, the one cure that never fails.

PURPORT

Youth is often blind and deaf to the warnings of oncoming old age and death. A passionate young person may think that such admonitions are for old-timers who do not know how to enjoy. Many so-called philosophers encourage this hedonistic attitude, which is precisely the attitude King Kulaśekhara is condemning in this verse. The hedonists advise, "Enjoy as much as you can while you're young, because you only live once." Not only is this advice morally unsound, but its premise is untrue: according to Vedic wisdom, our present life is only one in a series of innumerable lives we've experienced and will experience in innumerable bodies. Thus hedonism is a prescription for disaster, for the karmic reactions to a misspent youth will cause us to suffer in this lifetime and the next. In his poem *Śaraṇāgati,* Śrīla Bhaktivinoda Ṭhākura outlines the story of the conditioned soul who wastes a brief lifetime:

> I drank the deadly poison of worldliness, pretending it was nectar, and now the sun is setting on the horizon of my life. So soon has old age arrived and all happiness departed! Wracked by disease, troubled and weak, I find all my senses feeble now, my body wrecked and exhausted and my spirits downcast in the absence of youthful pleasures.
>
> Since I lack even a particle of devotion and am devoid of all enlightenment, what help is there for me now? Only You, O Lord, O

friend of the fallen, can help me. I am certainly fallen, the lowest of men. So please lift me up and place me at Your lotus feet.

King Kulaśekhara berates the foolish old person whose only response to his failing health is to seek some medicine. No medicine in the material world can prevent old age and disease, though modern allopathic medicine may temporarily cover the symptoms. The only medicine that can actually bring relief is the Kṛṣṇa elixir—Kṛṣṇa consciousness. It is sheer folly to turn solely to doctors in old age instead of to Kṛṣṇa.

One can see enlightenment among the elderly at pilgrimage sites in India, especially in Vṛndāvana. There one sees many old people visiting temples with intense devotion early in the morning. Hundreds of old people walk the circumambulation (*parikrama*) paths despite physical debilities. Some are bent nearly double! Someone might criticize that these people are not being provided with the Western medical treatment that could add a few years to their lives or ease their pain. But the sincere *bābājīs* and widows of Vṛndāvana who somehow make their way every morning to see Kṛṣṇa in the temples and who call out "Jaya Rādhe!" are actually fortunate and most intelligent. They are taking the *kṛṣṇa-rasāyana*, the elixir that will grant them eternal life in Kṛṣṇa's spiritual abode. The Vedic *śāstras* recommend that one drink this elixir from the beginning of life, but even if one neglects to do so earlier, one should by all means drink it during the waning days of life and thus cure the disease of repeated birth and death.

TEXT 38

आश्चर्यमेतद्धि मनुष्यलोके
सुधां परित्यज्य विषं पिबन्ति ।
नामानि नारायणगोचराणि
त्यक्त्वान्यवाचः कुहकाः पठन्ति ॥३८॥

āścaryam etad dhi manuṣya-loke
sudhāṁ parityajya viṣaṁ pibanti
nāmāni nārāyaṇa-gocarāṇi
tyaktvānya-vācaḥ kuhakāḥ paṭhanti

āścaryam—wonder; *etat*—this; *hi*—indeed; *manuṣya*—of human beings; *loke*—in the world; *sudhām*—life-giving nectar; *parityajya*—rejecting; *viṣam*—poison; *pibanti*—people drink; *nāmāni*—the names; *nārāyaṇa-gocarāṇi*—which refer to Lord Nārāyaṇa; *tyaktvā*—avoiding; *anya*—other; *vācaḥ*—words; *kuhakāḥ*—rogues; *paṭhanti*—they recite.

TRANSLATION

The greatest wonder in human society is this: People are so incorrigible that they reject the life-giving nectar of Lord Nārāyaṇa's names and instead drink poison by speaking everything else.

PURPORT

This verse reminds us of the verse in the *Mahābhārata* (*Vana-parva* 313.116) in which Mahārāja Yudhiṣṭhira answers this question from his father, Yamarāja: "What is the most amazing thing in the world?" Yudhiṣṭhira replies,

ahany ahani bhūtāni
gacchantīha yamālayam
śeṣāḥ sthāvaram icchanti
kim āścaryam ataḥ param

"Day after day countless living entities in this world go to the kingdom of death. Still, those who remain aspire for a permanent situation here. What could be more amazing than this?"

Both King Kulaśekhara and Mahārāja Yudhiṣṭhira use the word *āścaryam,* "amazing," in the sense of amazingly stupid. Yudhiṣṭhira is amazed that people can be so stupid and self-destructive that they refuse to recognize their impending deaths and thus misuse their brief human lives by failing to prepare for the next life. Kulaśekhara is amazed that people don't chant the holy names of God, although by this simple act they could gain eternal life. It is amazing that instead of blissfully drinking the nectar of the holy names, people drink the poison of worldly talk. As we have noted before, Śrīla Prabhupāda compared such worldly "chanting" to a frog's croaking, which attracts the snake—death.

One might argue that chanting the holy names is not *everything.*

Can't we also meditate on Brahman and discuss many worthy philosophical topics? Why does King Kulaśekhara condemn us just because we don't chant the names of God? The reason is that chanting the holy name has been directly given for all humanity as the *yuga-dharma,* the religion of the age. Spiritual methods such as *yoga* meditation were recommended for past millenniums, when conditions were more favorable. For this age, all Vedic scriptures and spiritual authorities have declared that chanting the holy names is the easiest method and also the topmost. To refuse it is stubbornness and foolishness

In 1970, when devotees of the Kṛṣṇa consciousness movement were publicly chanting *hari-nāma* daily in Berkeley, California, Dr. J. F. Staal, professor of philosophy and South Asian languages at the University of California, objected in a newspaper interview that the Kṛṣṇa consciousness movement was not bona fide because "[the devotees] spend too much time chanting to develop a philosophy." In an ensuing exchange of letters between Śrīla Prabhupāda and Dr. Staal, Prabhupāda quoted many scriptures to prove that chanting should be emphasized above all other practices for spiritual advancement. Dr. Staal had said that the *Bhagavad-gītā* does not recommend constant chanting, but Prabhupāda reminded him of verse 9.14, wherein Kṛṣṇa says about the *mahātmās,* or great souls: *satataṁ kīrtayanto mām.* "[They] are always chanting My glories."

Śrīla Prabhupāda quoted other verses from the *Bhagavad-gītā,* as well as from the *Śvetāśvatara Upaniṣad* and the *Nārada Pañcarātra,* confirming the importance of chanting the Hare Kṛṣṇa *mantra.* When the professor replied that he could also produce quotes to counter the Vedic conclusion, Prabhupāda agreed that the quoting could go back and forth forever without producing a conclusion. Therefore, Prabhupāda suggested, instead of arguing fruitlessly they should accept the judgment of an impeccable authority, such as Lord Caitanya. Śrīla Prabhupāda also pointed out that one could judge the effectiveness of chanting the holy names by seeing how young Westerners were becoming sanctified devotees of the Lord simply by following that process.

If speculative discussion on transcendental subjects is less valuable than chanting the holy names, then mundane talks are absolutely worthless. Unfortunately, most people are unaware that the goal of human life is liberation from birth and death. So they find nothing wrong in chattering away from morning till night on topics totally irrelevant to their liberation. The *ācāryas* give them innumerable warnings about the folly of wasting one's life in this way, and the material nature gives them many stiff lessons to teach them that finding permanent happiness here is a hopeless dream. But the "wonderful thing" is that people ignore their own mortality and refuse the life-giving nectar of the holy names in favor of the deadly poison of mundane talks.

TEXT 39

त्यजन्तु बान्धवाः सर्वे निन्दन्तु गुरवो जनाः ।
तथापि परमानन्दो गोविन्दो मम जीवनम् ॥३९॥

tyajantu bāndhavāḥ sarve
nindantu guravo janāḥ
tathāpi paramānando
govindo mama jīvanam

tyajantu—may they reject me; *bāndhavāḥ*—relatives; *sarve*—all; *nindantu*—may they condemn; *guravaḥ*—superior; *janāḥ*—persons; *tathā api*—nonetheless; *parama*—supreme; *ānandaḥ*—the embodiment of bliss; *govindaḥ*—Lord Govinda; *mama*—my; *jīvanam*—very life.

TRANSLATION

Let my relatives all abandon me and my superiors condemn me. Still, the supremely blissful Govinda remains my life and soul.

PURPORT

Ordinary people may condemn the Lord's devotees as ignorant fools, but the truly learned never do so. As Prahlāda Mahārāja states, "One who has dedicated his life to Kṛṣṇa through the nine methods of *bhakti* should be understood to be the most learned person, for he has acquired complete knowledge" (*Bhāg.* 7.5.24). But in the Kali-yuga, out of ignorance people mock the saintly devotees and praise demonic leaders in government, entertainment, and sports. Taking courage from the examples of saints like King Kulaśekhara and others, the devotees should not be ashamed when ordinary people disrespect them. They should be very concerned, however, that the Vaiṣṇavas and the Supreme Lord are pleased with their behavior.

Even the sage Nārada was condemned for his devotional activities: Dakṣa cursed him because he taught renunciation to Dakṣa's sons. Nārada remained tolerant, however, and continued traveling and preaching. The aim of Nārada and the devotees who follow his example is not to disrupt people's lives, but if their work is misunderstood, they must not abandon their duty but must continue their mission on behalf of the Lord. Śrīla Prabhupāda writes, "Because Nārada Muni and the members of his disciplic succession disrupt friendships and family life, they are sometimes accused of being *sauhṛda-ghna*, creators of enmity between relatives. Actually such devotees are friends of every living entity (*suhṛdaṁ sarva-bhūtānām*), but they are misunderstood to be enemies. Preaching can be a difficult, thankless task, but a preacher must follow the orders of the Supreme Lord and be unafraid of materialistic persons" (*Bhāg.* 6.5.39, purport). Conclusion: A devotee should remain happy executing his duty and not develop a "persecution complex."

The sentiment King Kulaśekhara expresses here is echoed by Mādhavendra Purī in one of his verses: "Let the sharp moralist accuse me of being illusioned; I do not mind. Experts in Vedic activities may slander me as being misled, friends and relatives may call me frustrated, my brothers may call me a fool, the wealthy mammonites may point me out as mad, and the learned philosophers may assert that I am much too proud. Still my mind does not budge an inch from the determination to serve the lotus feet of Govinda, though I am unable to do so."

TEXT 40

सत्यं ब्रवीमि मनुजाः स्वयमूर्ध्वबाहुर्
यो यो मुकुन्द नरसिंह जनार्दनेति ।
जीवो जपत्यनुदिनं मरणे रणे वा
पाषाणकाष्ठसदृशाय ददात्यभीष्टम् ॥४०॥

satyaṁ bravīmi manujāḥ svayam ūrdhva-bāhur
yo yo mukunda narasiṁha janārdaneti
jīvo japaty anu-dinaṁ maraṇe raṇe vā
pāṣāṇa-kāṣṭha-sadṛśāya dadāty abhīṣṭam

satyam—the truth; *bravīmi*—I am speaking; *manujāḥ*—O humans; *svayam*—myself; *ūrdhva*—with raised; *bāhuḥ*—arms; *yaḥ yaḥ*—whoever; *mukunda narasiṁha janārdana*—O Mukunda, Narasiṁha, Janārdana; *iti*—thus saying; *jīvaḥ*—a living being; *japati*—chants; *anu-dinam*—every day; *maraṇe*—at the time of death; *raṇe*—during battle; *vā*—or; *pāṣāṇa*—stone; *kāṣṭha*—or wood; *sadṛśāya*—to a state of similarity with; *dadāti*—he renders; *abhīṣṭam*—his cherished desires.

TRANSLATION

O mankind, with arms raised high I declare the truth! Any mortal who chants the names Mukunda, Nṛsiṁha, and Janārdana day after day, even in battle or when facing death, will come to regard his most cherished ambitions as no more valuable than a stone or a block of wood.

PURPORT

Even those who sincerely endeavor for self-improvement know that it is very hard to quell cherished ambitions. Sometimes these ambitions are so grandiose that we keep them secret, yet we cherish them within. An obscure, untalented man thinks he may one day become the dictator of the world. An unpublished poet dreams he will become the next Shakespeare. And so on. The materialists are always being encouraged to fan the fires of their ambition; even children are encouraged by their parents to "get ahead."

But pure devotees of the Lord are well aware that all worldly ambitions are useless. Śrīla Bhaktisiddhānta Sarasvatī Ṭhākura, to instruct us, criticizes his own mind and asks, "Why are you after fame? Don't you know it is as worthless as the dung of a boar?" Śrīla Raghunātha dāsa Gosvāmī uses an equally graphic metaphor to criticize *his* mind in his *Manaḥ-śikṣā,* comparing the desire for fame to a filthy dog-eater dancing in his heart. Devotees, then, must always be vigilant that the subtle desire for name, fame, and high position, technically called *pratiṣṭhāśā,* does not arise within the heart, since it blocks pure love for Kṛṣṇa from entering there.

In contrast to a devotee, an impersonalist finds it impossible to cleanse his heart completely of materialistic ambition. Even after he subdues some of the grosser ambitions, he still maintains the impossible wish to "become God." Śrīla Prabhupāda called this desire to become one in all respects with the Absolute Truth "the last snare of Māyā." And the demigods, in their prayers to Kṛṣṇa while He was still in the womb of Devakī, have given the last word on the impersonalists' so-called liberation of merging with the Absolute Truth:

ye 'nye 'ravindākṣa vimukta-māninas
tvayy asta-bhāvād aviśuddha-buddhayaḥ
āruhya kṛcchreṇa paraṁ padaṁ tataḥ
patanty adho 'nādṛta-yuṣmad-aṅghrayaḥ

"O lotus-eyed Lord, although nondevotees who accept severe austerities and penances to achieve the highest position may think themselves liberated, their intelligence is impure. They fall down from their position of imagined superiority because they have no regard for Your lotus feet" (*Bhāg.* 10.2.32).

King Kulaśekhara advises us how to rid ourselves of all material ambitions: We should chant the holy names of God—Mukunda, Nṛsiṁha, and Janārdana. These are all names of Kṛṣṇa, and as such they are contained within the *mahā-mantra:* Hare Krṣna, Hare Kṛṣṇa, Kṛṣṇa Kṛṣṇa, Hare Hare/ Hare Rāma, Hare Rāma, Rāma Rāma, Hare Hare. Chanting the names of Kṛṣṇa awakens one's love for Him, and then all one's material ambitions vanish. Śrīla Prabhupāda used to say that just as when someone gets a million dollars all his ten-dollar and hundred-dollar problems are automatically solved, so when we attain pure love for Kṛṣṇa all our petty material needs and desires pale to insignificance. Chanting the name of the Lord in pure ecstatic love puts the devotee in direct touch with the wonderful forms, qualities, and pastimes of the Lord; in that state the devotee is fully satisfied and loses all traces of egoistic ambition. He becomes happy simply to worship, serve, and be with the Supreme Personality of Godhead.

The history of Dhruva Mahārāja illustrates the purifying power of Kṛṣṇa consciousness. Dhruva sought out the Supreme Lord as a way to obtain a material kingdom. But after he had performed severe austerities and came face to face with Lord Viṣṇu, he declared, *svāmin kṛtārtho 'smi varaṁ na yāce:* "My dear Lord, I am fully satisfied. I do not ask from You any benediction for material sense gratification" (*Hari-bhakti-sudhodaya*).

Love of God is dormant within everyone, and to realize that love is to fulfill the purest ambition. The Vaiṣṇava *ācāryas* never advise us to try to kill our ambitious spirit; rather, they instruct us to desire only to awaken our taste for pure devotional service.

TEXT 41

नारायणाय नम इत्यमुमेव मन्त्रं
संसारघोरविषनिर्हरणाय नित्यम् ।
शृण्वन्तु भव्यमतयो यतयोऽनुरागाद्
उच्चैस्तरामुपदिशाम्यहमूर्ध्वबाहुः ॥४१॥

nārāyaṇāya nama ity amum eva mantraṁ
saṁsāra-ghora-viṣa-nirharaṇāya nityam
śṛṇvantu bhavya-matayo yatayo 'nurāgād
uccaistarām upadiśāmy aham ūrdhva-bāhuḥ

nārāyaṇāya namaḥ iti—"obeisances to Nārāyaṇa"; *amum*—this; *eva*—indeed; *mantram*—invocation; *saṁsāra*—of the cycle of material existence; *ghora*—terrible; *viṣa*—from the poison; *nirharaṇāya*—for deliverance; *nityam*—always; *śṛṇvantu*—they should hear; *bhavya*—good; *matayaḥ*—of intelligence; *yatayaḥ*—members of the renounced order; *anurāgāt*—out of love; *uccaiḥ-tarām*—very loudly; *upadiśāmi*—am advising; *aham*—I; *ūrdhva-bāhuḥ*—with arms raised.

TRANSLATION

Raising my arms, I utter this compassionate advice as loudly as I can: If those in the renounced order want to be delivered from the terrible, poisonous condition of material life, they should have the good sense to constantly hear the *mantra oṁ namo nārāyaṇāya.*

PURPORT

King Kulaśekhara addresses this verse to those who are renounced and also intelligent—two qualities essential for becoming fully Kṛṣṇa conscious.

As for renunciation, it is the basis of advancement on the path of *yoga.* In the *Bhagavad-gītā* (6.2) Lord Kṛṣṇa states, "What is called renunciation is the same as *yoga,* or linking oneself with the Supreme, for no one can become a *yogī* unless he renounces the desire for sense gratification." In Kulaśekhara's verse, the word *yatayaḥ,* translated as "members of the renounced order," refers not only to those who have formally accepted the *sannyāsa,* or mendicant, order, but to all those who have embraced the true spirit of renunciation. Kṛṣṇa defines *sannyāsa* as follows: "One who is unattached to the fruits of his work and who works as he is obligated is in the renounced order of life, and he is the true mystic, not he who lights no fire and performs no work" (Bg. 6.1). In other words, anyone who works solely for the pleasure of Kṛṣṇa, without a tinge of self-interest, has attained true renunciation.

Intelligence is also required to perform devotional service, especially to take up the chanting of the holy names. As Karabhājana Muni says to King Nimi in the *Śrīmad-Bhāgavatam* (11.5.32),

kṛṣṇa-varṇaṁ tviṣākṛṣṇaṁ sāṅgopāṅgāstra-pārṣadam
yajñair saṅkīrtana-prāyair yajanta hi su-medhasaḥ

"In the Age of Kali, intelligent persons perform congregational chanting of the holy names of God to worship the incarnation of Godhead who constantly sings the names of Kṛṣṇa. Although His complexion is not blackish, He is Kṛṣṇa Himself. He is accompanied by His associates, servants, weapons, and confidential companions."

Intelligence is not gauged by IQ examinations but by the ability to distinguish the permanent from the temporary, the true from the false, the good from the bad—and to act on that understanding. One can acquire such genuine intelligence only by hearing from a bona finde spiritual master and the authorized Vaiṣṇava scriptures. Then one will have the good sense to sacrifice immediate, temporary sense pleasures (*preyas*) in the interests of attaining the permanent good (*śreyas*): pure love of God and liberation from birth and death.

In the previous two verses King Kulaśekhara has expressed himself emphatically, raising his arms and chanting as loudly as he can. He has learned the most precious secret of existence and does not wish to hide it. That which is of such inestimable value—the *mantra* composed of the names of God—should not be kept secret. People should not be denied access to it, even if they seem unqualified. Once the *ācārya* Rāmānuja was given a secret *mantra* by his *guru,* who told him that revealing it would be detrimental to his spiritual advancement. But Rāmānuja loudly chanted the potent *mantra* and taught it to the people in general. When his *guru* asked him why he had done this, Rāmānuja said that if the *mantra* was beneficial, then he wished to give it to everyone, even at the risk of going to hell. This mood is reflected in Lord Caitanya and His *saṅkīrtana* movement: "Not considering who asked for it and who did not, and who is fit and who is unfit to receive it, Caitanya Mahāprabhu distributed the fruit of devotional service" (Cc. *Ādi* 9.29.36).

Especially in the present age, most people do not have sufficient good *karma* to attain renunciation or higher intelligence. And yet every living entity, being a pure spirit soul, originally has all good qualities. The *ācāryas* and preachers help conditioned souls bring out their dormant good qualities by inducing them to chant the holy names. Again and again King Kulaśekhara recommends *hari-nāma,* in the form of both congregational chanting (*saṅkīrtana*) and individual meditative chanting (*japa*). There are no hard and fast rules for chanting the holy names of the Lord, but what *is* a hard and fast rule, especially in this age, is that everyone must take part in calling on God by His innumerable names.

TEXT 42

चित्तं नैव निवर्तते क्षणमपि श्रीकृष्णपादाम्बुजान्
निन्दन्तु प्रियबान्धवा गुरुजना गृह्णन्तु मुञ्चन्तु वा ।
दुर्वादं परिघोषयन्तु मनुजा वंशे कलङ्कोऽस्तु वा
तादृक्प्रेमधरानुरागमधुना मत्ताय मानं तु मे ॥४२॥

cittaṁ naiva nivartate kṣaṇam api śrī-kṛṣṇa-pādāmbujān
nindantu priya-bāndhavā guru-janā gṛhṇantu muñcantu vā

durvādaṁ parighoṣayantu manujā vaṁśe kalaṅko 'stu vā
tādṛk-prema-dharānurāga-madhunā mattāya mānaṁ tu me

cittam—the mind; *na eva*—never; *nivartate*—turns away; *kṣaṇam api*—even for a moment; *śrī-kṛṣṇa-pāda-ambujāt*—from the lotus feet of Śrī Kṛṣṇa; *nindantu*—let them criticize; *priya*—dear ones; *bāndhavāḥ*—and other relatives; *guru-janāḥ*—superior; *gṛhṇantu*—let them accept; *muñcantu*—reject; *vā*—or; *durvādam*—calumniation; *parighoṣayantu*—let them proclaim; *manujāḥ*—people; *vaṁśe*—on the family; *kalaṅkaḥ*—a dirty spot; *astu*—let there be; *vā*—or; *tādṛk*—such as this; *prema*—of love of Godhead; *dharā*—the abundance; *anurāga*—of sentiments of attractions; *madhunā*—with the sweet honey; *mattāya*—who is maddened; *mānam*—respect; *tu*—however; *me*—for me.

TRANSLATION

My mind cannot turn from Śrī Kṛṣṇa's lotus feet, even for a moment. So let my dear ones and other relatives criticize me, my superiors accept or reject me as they like, the common people spread evil gossip about me, and my family's reputation be sullied. For a madman like me, it is honor enough to feel this flood of love of Godhead, which brings such sweet emotions of attraction for my Lord.

PURPORT

King Kulaśekhara again expresses his lack of concern about suffering ill repute due to his intense devotion to Lord Kṛṣṇa. If devotional service resulted in such criticism hundreds of years ago in India, then how much more calumny must devotees undergo in modern countries that have no heritage of worshiping at the lotus feet of Śrī Kṛṣṇa! Therefore King Kulaśekhara gives us a realistic warning—and assurance not to be afraid of criticism.

When Lord Kṛṣṇa enjoyed His pastimes in Vṛndāvana five thousand years ago, the *gopīs,* His dearmost devotees, also risked their reputations to serve Him. In the middle of the full-moon night of the autumn season, He called the *gopīs* by playing His transcendental flute, and they all rushed out to meet Him. Disregarding the commands of their husbands, brothers, and other relatives, ignoring such duties as suckling their children and cooking, they broke all the bonds of Vedic propriety and went to meet their lover, Kṛṣṇa. The Lord very much appreciated this daring sacrifice by the *gopīs*. As stated in *Caitanya-caritāmṛta*, "The *gopīs* have forsaken everything, including their own relatives and their punishment and scolding, for the sake of serving Lord Kṛṣṇa. They render loving service to Him for the sake of His enjoyment" (Cc. *Ādi* 4.169).

A devotee knows that he is pleasing Lord Kṛṣṇa when he pleases the representative of Kṛṣṇa, and also when he feels spiritual satisfaction (*yenātmā su-prasīdati*). At that time he doesn't care about any volume of worldly criticism. When a surrendered devotee faces slights and ostracism, these simply help crush any lingering desire he may have to enjoy the company of family and friends. In this way Kṛṣṇa severs the worldly ties of His devotee and brings him entirely under His control and within His shelter.

King Kulaśekhara tells us why he can endure criticism without much pain: He is feeling an abundance of love of Godhead, accompanied by varieties of ecstatic emotions, and he considers this to be so wonderful and honorable that he can easily tolerate the petty insults of nondevotees. This kind of indifference is the effect of advancement in chanting the holy names, as explained in the following verse from *Śrīmad-Bhāgavatam* (11.2.40), which Lord Caitanya says embodies the essence of the *Bhāgavatam's* teachings:

evaṁ-vrataḥ sva-priya-nāma-kīrtyā
jātānurāgo druta-citta uccaiḥ
hasaty atho roditi rauti gāyaty
unmāda-van nṛtyati loka-bāhyaḥ

"By chanting the holy name of the Supreme Lord, one comes to the stage of love of Godhead. Then the devotee is fixed in his vow as an eternal servant of the Lord, and he gradually becomes very much attached to a particular name and form of the Supreme Personality of Godhead. As his heart melts with ecstatic love, he laughs very loudly or cries or shouts. Sometimes he sings and dances like a madman, for he is indifferent to public opinion."

TEXT 43

कृष्णो रक्षतु नो जगत्त्रयगुरुः कृष्णं नमध्वं सदा
कृष्णेनाखिलशत्रवो विनिहताः कृष्णाय तस्मै नमः ।
कृष्णादेव समुत्थितं जगदिदं कृष्णस्य दासोऽस्म्यहं
कृष्णे तिष्ठति विश्वमेतदखिलं हे कृष्ण रक्षस्व माम् ॥४३॥

kṛṣṇo rakṣatu no jagat-traya-guruḥ kṛṣṇaṁ namadhvaṁ sadā
kṛṣṇenākhila-śatravo vinihatāḥ kṛṣṇāya tasmai namaḥ
kṛṣṇād eva samutthitaṁ jagad idaṁ kṛṣṇasya dāso 'smy ahaṁ
kṛṣṇe tiṣṭhati viśvam etad akhilaṁ he kṛṣṇa rakṣasva mām

kṛṣṇaḥ—Kṛṣṇa; *rakṣatu*—may He protect; *naḥ*—us; *jagat*—of the worlds; *traya*—three; *guruḥ*—the spiritual master; *kṛṣṇam*—to Kṛṣṇa; *namadhvam*—all of you bow down; *sadā*—constantly; *kṛṣṇena*—by Kṛṣṇa; *akhila*—all; *śatravaḥ*—enemies; *vinihatāḥ*—killed; *kṛṣṇāya*—to Kṛṣṇa; *tasmai*—Him; *namaḥ*—obeisances; *kṛṣṇāt*—from Kṛṣṇa; *eva*—alone; *samutthitam*—risen; *jagat*—world; *idam*—this; *kṛṣṇasya*—of Kṛṣṇa; *dāsaḥ*—the servant; *asmi*—am; *aham*—I; *kṛṣṇe*—in Kṛṣṇa; *tiṣṭhati*—stands; *viśvam*—universe; *etat*—this; *akhilam*—entire; *he kṛṣṇa*—O Kṛṣṇa; *rakṣasva mām*—protect me.

TRANSLATION

May Kṛṣṇa, the spiritual master of the three worlds, protect us. Continually bow down to Kṛṣṇa. Kṛṣṇa has killed all our enemies. Obeisances to Kṛṣṇa. From Kṛṣṇa alone this world has come into being. I am the servant of Kṛṣṇa. This entire universe rests within Kṛṣṇa. O Kṛṣṇa, please protect me!

PURPORT

Gopīparāṇadhana Prabhu notes, "This verse uses each of the eight grammatical cases of the word Kṛṣṇa, one after another." By this Kṛṣṇa-ized Sanskrit composition, the poet reveals various ways to approach

Lord Kṛṣṇa's name and pastimes.

This verse is reminiscent of how Lord Caitanya (then known as Nimāi Paṇḍita) taught Sanskrit grammar when He was a sixteen-year-old schoolmaster. He opened His own *catuṣ-pāṭhī* (village school) in the area of Navadvīpa, and at first He would teach grammar in the traditional way. But after returning from Gaya, where He received initiation from Śrīla Īśvara Purī, He would simply explain Kṛṣṇa in all the readings of grammar. Śrīla Prabhupāda writes, "In order to please Lord Caitanya, Śrīla Jīva Gosvāmī later composed a grammar in Sanskrit in which all the rules of the grammar are exemplified with the holy names of the Lord. This grammar is still current and is known as *Hari-nāmāmṛta-vyākaraṇa* and is prescribed by the syllabus of Sanskrit schools in Bengal even today" (*Śrīmad-Bhāgavatam* Introduction).

Here King Kulaśekhara addresses Lord Kṛṣṇa as the spiritual master of the three worlds, the killer of enemies, and the creator and maintainer of the universe. Although the Supreme Lord appoints intermediaries to represent Him as *guru,* protector, creator, and maintainer, Lord Kṛṣṇa is the ultimate person behind all those who act on His behalf. The bona fide initiating and instructing *gurus* faithfully carry the message of the original *guru,* the Supreme Personality of Godhead. Also, the Lord is a *guru* in a more direct sense, since He personally becomes a spiritual master for any aspiring devotee, even today, through His teachings in the *Bhagavad-gītā.* And as the *caitya-guru,* the spiritual master within the heart, He is also the personal inner guide for every living being. In a similar way, Lord Kṛṣṇa protects all *jīvas* as Mahā-Viṣṇu when they merge into Him at the time of universal annihilation, and He kills demons for the benefit of all human beings when He appears in His various *avatāras.*

Although one should not expect the Lord to come running to protect us or teach us, as if *He* were *our* servant, a sincere devotee should expect Kṛṣṇa's guidance and protection—and also accept them in whatever form they come. The standard method of receiving Kṛṣṇa's instructions and protection is through the *paramparā,* or disciplic succession, which embodies the combined potency of *guru, śāstra,* and *sādhu* (the spiritual master, the scriptures, and the saintly devotees). Therefore we may all call out directly to the Lord, "O Kṛṣṇa, please protect me!" and receive His mercy in *paramparā.*

TEXT 44

हे गोपालक हे कृपाजलनिधे हे सिन्धुकन्यापते
हे कंसान्तक हे गजेन्द्रकरुणापारीण हे माधव ।
हे रामानुज हे जगत्त्रयगुरो हे पुण्डरीकाक्ष मां
हे गोपीजननाथ पालय परं जानामि न त्वां विना ॥४४॥

he gopālaka he kṛpā-jala-nidhe he sindhu-kanyā-pate
he kaṁsāntaka he gajendra-karuṇā-pārīṇa he mādhava
he rāmānuja he jagat-traya-guro he puṇḍarīkākṣa mām
he gopījana-nātha pālaya paraṁ jānāmi na tvāṁ vinā

he gopālaka—O cowherd boy; *he*—O; *kṛpā*—of mercy; *jala-nidhe*—ocean; *he*—O; *sindhu*—of the ocean; *kanyā*—of the daughter (goddess Lakṣmī, who took birth from the Milk Ocean); *pate*—husband; *he kaṁsa-antaka*—O killer of Kaṁsa; *he*—O; *gaja-indra*—to the king of the elephants; *karuṇā*—with mercy; *pārīṇa*—full; *he mādhava*—O Lord Mādhava; *he rāma-anuja*—O younger brother of Lord Balarāma; *he*—O; *jagat-traya*—of the three worlds; *guro*—spiritual master; *he*—O; *puṇḍarīka-akṣa*—lotus-eyed one; *mām*—me; *he*—O; *gopī-jana*—of the cowherd women of Vraja; *nātha*—master; *pālaya*—please protect; *param*—supreme; *jānāmi na*—I do not know; *tvām vinā*—other than You.

TRANSLATION

O young cowherd boy! O ocean of mercy! O husband of Lakṣmī, the ocean's daughter! O killer of Kaṁsa! O merciful benefactor of Gajendra! O Mādhava! O younger brother of Rāma! O spiritual master of the three worlds! O lotus-eyed Lord of the *gopīs*! I know no one greater than You. Please protect me.

PURPORT

King Kulaśekhara's prayers are all addressed to the Supreme Personality of Godhead in His various expansions and incarnations. Sometimes he addresses Lord Nārāyaṇa or Lord Rāma, but very frequently he specifies Lord Kṛṣṇa as his object of special attraction. According to the *Śrīmad-Bhagavatam* (1.3.28), Lord Kṛṣṇa is in fact the source of all incarnations and expansions:

ete cāṁśa-kalāḥ puṁsaḥ kṛṣṇas tu bhagavān svayam
indrāri-vyākulaṁ lokaṁ mṛḍayanti yuge yuge

"All [these] incarnations are either plenary portions or portions of the plenary portions of the Lord, but Lord Śrī Kṛṣṇa is the original Personality of Godhead Himself. In every age He protects the world through His different features when the world is disturbed by the enemies of Indra" (*Bhāg.* 1.3.28).

In his famous "Govinda Prayers" in the *Brahma-saṁhitā,* Lord Brahmā teaches this same conclusive truth, or *siddhānta*—namely, that all incarnations of Godhead and all demigods, as well as all the material and spiritual worlds and their constitutional elements, originate from Lord Kṛṣṇa, or Govinda: *govindam ādi-puruṣaṁ tam ahaṁ bhajāmi.*

In Text 43 King Kulaśekhara directly used the name Kṛṣṇa nine times, while in the present verse he calls on Kṛṣṇa by names that refer to His pastimes. The names in this verse are all as good as the name Kṛṣṇa, since they all arise from *kṛṣṇa-līlā,* in which the Lord is known variously as Gopāla (a cowherd boy), as Kaṁsāntaka (the killer of Kaṁsa), as Rāmānuja (the younger brother of Balarāma), or as Gopījananātha (the Lord of the *gopīs*). Ultimately, all names of God refer to Kṛṣṇa. For a Kṛṣṇa devotee, whether God is addressed by the name Kṛṣṇa or other names—even names of God from other religions—the devotee, following the conclusion of the *Śrīmad-Bhāgavatam* and the *Brahma-saṁhitā,* always understands that these names ultimately designate the Supreme Personality of Godhead, Kṛṣṇa.

In this verse we also see a combination of personal devotion and objective appreciation of the Lord. One often finds this in the Vaiṣṇava poetry of the Ālvārs of South India, of whom Kulaśekhara is one. Within a few lines the *bhakta* will praise the Lord for some of His inconceivable, awe-inspiring activities—and then exclaim how this same great Lord is his personal Lord in the heart.

King Kulaśekhara addresses Lord Kṛṣṇa as the spiritual master of the three worlds, and he calls upon the Lord to protect him. One may question, "Since Lord Viṣṇu is already protecting all living beings, why should a devotee ask for personal protection?" But the *bhakta* is not seeking physical protection; he wants his personal loving relationship with the Lord to be nourished and maintained. In other words, he wants the Lord to protect him from the greatest calamity—forgetfulness of Him.

Śrīla Prabhupāda explains, "The Lord, the Supreme Personality of Godhead, is already in charge of the maintenance of this creation by virtue of His plenary expansion Kṣīrodakśāyī Viṣṇu, but this maintenance is not direct. However, when the Lord says that He takes charge of His pure devotee, He actually takes direct charge" (*Caitanya-caritāmṛta,* Preface). The pure devotee is one who surrenders to the Lord just as a child surrenders to his parents or an animal to its master. When a devotee submits himself in that way, Kṛṣṇa gives him special attention and protection. King Kulaśekhara praises the Lord according to the *śāstra* and according to His *līlā,* and yet he also calls upon Him for personal protection, confident that the Lord will fulfill His promise to reciprocate with all His devotees according to how they approach Him.

TEXT 45

दारा वाराकरवरसुता ते तनूजो विरिञ्चिः
स्तोता वेदस्तव सुरगणा भृत्यवर्गः प्रसादः ।
मुक्तिर्माया जगदविकलं तावकी देवकी ते
माता मित्रं बलरिपुसुतस्तत्त्वदन्यं न जाने ॥४५॥

dārā vār-ākara-vara-sutā te tanūjo viriñciḥ
stotā vedas tava sura-gaṇā bhṛtya-vargaḥ prasādaḥ
muktir māyā jagad avikalaṁ tāvakī devakī te
mātā mitraṁ bala-ripu-sutas tat tvad anyaṁ na jāne

dārā—wife; *vāḥ-ākara*—of the ocean; *vara*—excellent; *sutā*—the daughter (Lakṣmī); *te*—Your; *tanūjaḥ*—son; *viriñciḥ*—Lord Brahmā; *stotā*—praiser; *vedaḥ*—the *Vedas; tava*—Your; *sura-gaṇāḥ*—the demigods; *bhṛtya*—of servants; *vargaḥ*—company; *prasādaḥ*—grace; *muktiḥ*—liberation; *māyā*—magic power; *jagat*—the universe; *avikalam*—entire;

tāvakī—Your; *devakī*—Devakī; *te*—Your; *mātā*—mother; *mitram*—friend; *bala-ripu*—(Indra) the enemy of the demon Bala; *sutaḥ*—the son (Arjuna); *tat*—thus; *tvat*—than You; *anyam*—any other; *na jāne*—I do not know.

TRANSLATION

Your wife is the beautiful daughter of the ocean, and Your son is Lord Brahmā. The *Vedas* are Your panegyrist, the demigods comprise Your company of servants, and liberation is Your benediction, while this entire universe is a display of Your magic power. Śrīmatī Devakī is Your mother, and Arjuna, the son Indra, is Your friend. For these reasons I have no interest in anyone but You.

PURPORT

Even an ordinary man may have a daughter and a son; a famous man will have so many people praising him (or he may hire press agents to do so); and a powerful political leader will have less powerful political figures as his official servants. The Supreme Personality of Godhead is also a person, and therefore He also has family members, as well as servants, friends, and praisers. Since the Absolute Truth is the source of everything (*janmādy asya yataḥ*), we should not think He lacks anything we see in the material world. But when the Supreme Lord, Kṛṣṇa, manifests personal relationships, they are not ordinary: His wife, friends, servants, and praisers are all liberated souls, His personal energies, or expansions of Himself.

People doubt that God can have a father, mother, wife, or special friend. Some say that these relationships compromise the impartiality and unchangeability of the Supreme. But the Lord's transcendental relationships with His eternal associates do not compromise Him in any way. Rather, they add to His ever-increasing glory. Lord Kṛṣṇa does not actually need any of His friends, wives, and so on, but He allows them to associate with Him intimately because He is always pleased to reciprocate with loving devotees.

That the Lord's associates are not ordinary is proved by the fact that they often undergo extreme austerities or great sacrifices to become His friends or parents. For example, Vasudeva and Devakī, who took the role of Kṛṣṇa's father and mother, executed many lifetimes of austerity in preparation. Soon after His birth, Kṛṣṇa described to them what they had undergone in a previous life to receive the benediction of having Him as their son:

> Both of you practiced severe austerities for twelve thousand years by the calculation of the demigods. During that time, your mind was always absorbed in Me. When you were executing devotional service and always thinking of Me within your heart, I was very much pleased with you. O sinless mother, your heart is therefore always pure. At that time I also appeared before you in this form just to fulfill your desire, and I asked you to ask whatever you desired. At that time you wished to have Me born as your son. [*Kṛṣṇa, the Supreme Personality of Godhead,* p. 53]

In His spiritual kingdom the Supreme Lord eternally enjoys loving relationships with His personal associates, but He is also present in all nooks and crannies of the material universes and in everyone's heart. In this way His influence is spread throughout all existence, both spiritual and material. Thus King Kulaśekhara says, "This entire universe is a display of Your magic power." Lord Kṛṣṇa is not a minor magician. He is Yogeśvara, the controller of all mystic potencies. In the *Bhagavad-gītā* (5.29), Lord Kṛṣṇa declares, *sarva-loka-maheśvaram:* "I am the supreme controller of all universes." Moreover, Kṛṣṇa controls all the universes effortlessly. As Śrīla Prabhupāda says, we should not think He is like Atlas, whom we see struggling to hold up the earth on his arms. Kṛṣṇa always has free time to enjoy with His loving associates.

"For all these reasons," declares King Kulaśekhara, "I have no interest in anyone but You."

TEXT 46

प्रणाममीशस्य शिरःफलं विदु-
स्तदर्चनं प्राणफलं दिवौकसः ।
मनःफलं तद्गुणतत्त्वचिन्तनं
वचःफलं तद्गुणकीर्तनं बुधाः ॥४६॥

praṇāmam īśasya śiraḥ-phalaṁ vidus
tad-arcanaṁ prāṇa-phalaṁ divaukasaḥ
manaḥ-phalaṁ tad-guṇa-tattva-cintanaṁ
vacaḥ-phalaṁ tad-guṇa-kīrtanaṁ budhāḥ

praṇāmam—offering obeisances; *īśasya*—to the Supreme Lord; *śiraḥ*—of the head; *phalam*—the perfection; *viduḥ*—they know; *tat*—His; *arcanam*—worship; *prāṇa*—of one's breath; *phalam*—the perfection; *diva-okasaḥ*—the residents of heaven; *manaḥ*—of the mind; *phalam*—the perfection; *tat*—His; *guṇa*—of the qualities; *tattva*—on the details; *cintanam*—meditation; *vacaḥ*—of speech; *phalam*—the perfection; *tat*—His; *guṇa*—about the qualities; *kīrtanam*—chanting; *budhāḥ*—intelligent.

TRANSLATION

The wise inhabitants of the heavenly regions know that the perfection of the head is to offer prostrate obeisances to the Supreme Lord, the perfection of the life-breath is to worship the Lord, the perfection of the mind is to ponder the details of His transcendental qualities, and the perfection of speech is to chant the glories of His qualities.

PURPORT

The word *divaukasaḥ* refers to the *devas,* or demigods. These are devotees of the Supreme Lord who inhabit the heavenly planets and enjoy a rare standard of sense gratification, which places them squarely within the material world as conditioned souls. But because they are staunch followers of Lord Viṣṇu, He always protects them. Being Viṣṇu's followers, they are usually victorious in their battles with the demons, who frequently threaten to possess the heavenly kingdom.

King Kulaśekhara mentions the *devas* not because of their material opulence but because of their good quality of rendering devotional service to Lord Hari. The residents of the heavenly planets are not like the people of the earth, where, in Kali-yuga, the philosophy of "God is dead" predominates and the ideas of atheists like Darwin, Marx, and Freud are hugely influential in all affairs. Although the *devas* have access to very advanced forms of technology and possess mystic powers, their faith in Lord Viṣṇu remains pure.

By the grace of Lord Caitanya, even the people of the earth planet, although unqualified in many ways, can also approach Lord Kṛṣṇa in devotional service. Indeed, Lord Caitanya is so magnanimous that He has given the residents of earth a great advantage over the demigods. That advantage is *saṅkīrtana,* the congregational chanting of the holy names of God. Because of this great advantage, the earth is the best place to achieve the ultimate goal of life, going back to the eternal spiritual world. As stated in the *Śrīmad-Bhāgavatam* (5.19.21),

> Since the human form of life is the sublime position for spiritual realization, all the demigods in heaven speak in this way: "How wonderful it is for these human beings to have been born in the land of Bhārata-varṣa [the earth]! They must have executed pious acts of austerity in the past, or the Supreme Personality of Godhead Himself must have been pleased with them. Otherwise, how could they engage in devotional service in so many ways? We demigods can only aspire to achieve human births in Bhārata-varṣa to execute devotional service, but these human beings are already engaged there."

At one time the whole world was known as Bhārata-varṣa, but now only India is known by that name. India is cited as the best place to achieve self-realization because it was in India that many *ācāryas* and incarnations of Kṛṣṇa appeared, and it is in India that the tradition of devotional service to the Lord remains strong. Śrīla Prabhupāda writes, "From all points of view, Bhārata-varṣa is the special land where one can very easily understand the process of devotional service and adopt it to make his life successful." Lord Caitanya has further encouraged the residents of Bhārata-varṣa to make themselves successful in devotional service and then preach throughout the world. This is the work of the Kṛṣṇa consciousness movement, a mission that was developed so thoroughly and successfully by His Divine Grace A. C. Bhaktivedanta Swami Prabhupāda.

King Kulaśekhara reminds us of the proper functions of the various parts of the body. The head, for instance, is the center of all the senses, so we try to give it pleasure in many ways, but usually not by the humble act recommended here—bowing down before the Supreme Lord. Of course, bowing is not merely a mechanical act: the head should bow down accompanied by sincere feelings of devotion in the heart. Prostrating the body was an important part of the daily *sādhana* (discipline) of liberated souls like the six Gosvāmīs of Vṛndāvana. In his prayers to the six Gosvāmīs, Śrīnivāsa Ācārya states that they were "engaged in chanting the holy names of the Lord and bowing down in a scheduled measurement." Raghunātha dāsa Gosvāmī, one of the six Gosvāmīs, offered one thousand obeisances to the Lord's devotees daily.

The word *prāṇa,* used in this verse of *Mukunda-mālā-stotra,* refers to the life-breath, which we should used in worshiping the Lord. *Yogīs* practice *prāṇāyāma,* regulation of the breath, to gain control of the mind and senses, and it is often recommended as a method of rejuvenation. Although one may certainly gain such benefits by controlling the breath, the path of *bhakti* calls on the devotee simply to use his life-breath in loving service to the Lord. Similarly, we should use the mind, speech, and all our other God-given faculties in the Lord's loving service. This perfection is available to all, whether demigods or human beings.

TEXT 47

श्रीमन्नाम प्रोच्य नारायणाख्यं
के न प्रापुर्वाञ्छितं पापिनोऽपि ।
हा नः पूर्वं वाक् प्रवृत्ता न तस्मिंस्
तेन प्राप्तं गर्भवासादिदुःखम् ॥४७॥

śrīman-nāma procya nārāyaṇākhyaṁ
ke na prāpur vāñchitaṁ pāpino 'pi
hā naḥ pūrvaṁ vāk pravṛttā na tasmiṁs
tena prāptaṁ garbha-vāsādi-duḥkham

śrīmat—blessed; *nāma*—the name; *procya*—having said out loud; *nārāyaṇa-ākhyam*—called "Nārāyaṇa"; *ke*—who; *na prāpuḥ*—did not obtain; *vāñchitam*—what they desired; *pāpinaḥ*—sinful persons; *api*—even; *hā*—alas; *naḥ*—our; *pūrvam*—previously; *vāk*—speech; *pravṛttā*—engaged; *na*—not; *tasmin*—in that; *tena*—therefore; *prāptam*—achieved; *garbha*—in a womb; *vāsa*—residence; *ādi*—beginning with; *duḥkham*—misery.

TRANSLATION

What person, even if most sinful, has ever said aloud the blessed name Nārāyaṇa and failed to fulfill his desires? But we, alas, never used our power of speech in that way, and so we had to suffer such miseries as living in a womb.

PURPORT

This verse brings to mind the story of Ajāmila from the *Śrīmad-Bhagavatam.* Ajāmila was sinful, but by chanting the name Nārāyaṇa when on the verge of death, he fulfilled his ultimate desires. In the following quotation from the *Bhāgavatam* (6.2.13), Lord Viṣṇu's servants explain to the servants of Yamarāja, the lord of death, why Ajāmila is not a fit candidate for punishment:

"At the time of his death this Ajāmila helplessly and very loudly chanted the holy name of the Lord, Nārāyaṇa. That chanting alone has already freed him from the reactions of all sinful life. Therefore, O servants of Yamarāja, do not try to take him to your master for punishment in hellish conditions."

Ajāmila had chanted indirectly, calling out the name of his son, but because he uttered the holy name Nārāyaṇa he was saved from hell. He then went on to perfect his Kṛṣṇa consciousness and return home, back to Godhead. His "accidental" chanting of the holy name, therefore, awakened his original desire to serve the Lord. If even an extremely sinful person like Ajāmila could be saved by chanting the name Nārāyaṇa indirectly, then no one else should fail to achieve his utmost desires by chanting the blessed name Nārāyaṇa.

King Kulaśekhara speaks on behalf of all those who forget to chant the holy names. These verses are meant for all of us who are missing the opportunity of achieving perfection through chanting. If we do not call on the Supreme Lord, then we will have to face all kinds of miseries. Kulaśekhara mentions the pain of living in the womb. Lord Kapila provides graphic details of that ordeal in His teachings to His mother, Devahūti:

> Bitten again and again all over the body by the hungry worms in the abdomen itself, the child suffers terrible agony. Because of his tenderness he thus becomes unconscious moment after moment

because of the terrible condition.

Then owing to the mother's eating bitter, pungent foods, or food which is too salty or too sour, the body of the child incessantly suffers pains which are almost intolerable. [*Bhāg.* 3.31.7–8]

People refuse to recognize these facts, and that is one reason they do not take shelter of the holy name. Even if they are reminded of the pains they suffered in the past, they claim that it doesn't matter now because they are free from the pain. But a person who disregards natural and scriptural law guarantees that he will suffer the same torments he claims to have forgotten. Śrīla Prabhupāda writes, "One who does not take heed of these indications of suffering in human existence is said to be undoubtedly committing suicide" (*Bhāg.* 7.31.9, purport).

Vaiṣṇava poetry is filled with Vedic truths and can bring the utmost benefit, as well as pleasure to the ear and heart. In this single *śloka* King Kulaśekhara has given us a poignant description of our unfortunate predicament, with a hint of hope for ultimate salvation. If we can grasp the message of even this one verse—and also feel it and act upon it—then we can save ourselves unlimited grief.

TEXT 48

ध्यायन्ति ये विष्णुमनन्तमव्ययं
हृत्पद्ममध्ये सततं व्यवस्थितम् ।
समाहितानां सतताभयप्रदं
ते यान्ति सिद्धिं परमां तु वैष्णवीम् ॥४८॥

dhyāyanti ye viṣṇum anantam avyayaṁ
hṛt-padma-madhye satataṁ vyavasthitam
samāhitānāṁ satatābhaya-pradaṁ
te yānti siddhiṁ paramāṁ tu vaiṣṇavīm

dhyāyanti—meditate; *ye*—who; *viṣṇum*—on Lord Viṣṇu; *anantam*—the unlimited; *avyayam*—the infallible; *hṛt*—of the heart; *padma*—the lotus; *madhye*—within; *satatam*—always; *vyavasthitam*—situated; *samāhitānām*—for those who are fixed in awareness of Him; *satata*—

perpetual; *abhaya*—fearlessness; *pradam*—granting; *te*—they; *yānti*—attain; *siddhim*—perfection; *paramām*—supreme; *tu*—indeed; *vaiṣṇavīm*—of the Vaiṣṇavas, and in relation to Viṣṇu.

TRANSLATION

The unlimited and infallible Viṣṇu, who is always present within the lotus of the heart, grants fearlessness to those who fix their intelligence upon Him. The devotees who meditate on Him will reach the supreme perfection of the Vaiṣṇavas.

PURPORT

King Kulaśekhara has previously spoken of perfections we can attain by using our mind and senses in the service of the Supreme Lord. Now he specifies that the ultimate perfection is *siddhiṁ vaiṣṇavīm,* the supreme perfection of the Vaiṣṇavas.

All Vaiṣṇavas are rightly situated, but even among devotees there are progressive states. In *The Nectar of Devotion,* Śrīla Prabhupāda summarizes the characteristics of three classes of devotees. We paraphrase his summary as follows: The third-class devotee is one whose faith is not strong and who, at the same time, does not recognize the decision of the revealed scriptures. The second-class devotee may not be expert in arguing on the basis of scripture, but he has firm faith in the objective. And the first-class devotee is one who is very expert in the study and explanation of the scriptures and at the same time has strong faith.

For the most part, the third-class devotee (known as *kaniṣṭha-adhikārī*) has faith in the Deity in the temple and worships the Lord there. But the *kaniṣṭha-adhikārī* is usually unable to appreciate other devotees or the presence of the Lord in everyone's heart. Nevertheless, even the third-class Vaiṣṇava is considered highly elevated. Śrīla Prabhupāda writes, "Even the third-class devotee—who is not advanced in knowledge of the Absolute Truth but simply offers obeisances with great devotion, thinks of the Lord, sees the Lord in the temple, and brings flowers and fruit to offer to the Deity—becomes imperceptibly liberated" (*Bhāg.* 3.25.36, purport). By dint of his attraction to the Deities of Śrī Śrī Rādhā-Kṛṣṇa or Lakṣmī-Nārāyaṇa, the *kaniṣṭha-adhikārī* is in a transcendental position, above those who are trying for liberation by speculation or other methods.

One advances through the stages of perfection by applying oneself under the direction of the *guru*—and everything depends on one's faith. In the *Caitanya-caritāmṛta* (*Madhya* 22.64), Lord Caitanya confirms this, explaining to Sanātana Gosvāmī that one becomes qualified as a devotee on the elementary platform, the intermediate platform, and the highest platform of devotional service according to the development of one's *śraddhā* (faith).

One does not advance in devotional service as one does in the material world, by climbing up a social ladder or by working hard for economic development or by military strength. Rather, one has to give up all material "strengths" and designations and become as humble as a blade of grass. The basis of devotional service is chanting of the holy name, and according to Lord Caitanya one cannot chant constantly unless one offers all respects to others without expecting respect for oneself. Instead of trying to push oneself ahead while maintaining the contaminations of lust, anger, and greed in the heart, one has to become pure and realize oneself as the servant of God, His devotees, and all living beings.

The perfect stage of devotion is described in Text 25 of the *Mukunda-mālā-stotra:* "O enemy of Madhu and Kaiṭabha, O Lord of the universe, the perfection of my life and the most cherished mercy You could show me would be for You to consider me the servant of the servant of the servant of the servant of the servant of the servant of Your servant." Lord Caitanya also expressed this important sentiment when He declared that He was not a *brāhmaṇa* or a *sannyāsī* but a servant of the servant of the servant of the lotus feet of Kṛṣṇa, the Lord of the *gopīs* of Vṛndāvana. Thus devotees who want to attain devotional perfections will pray for the good fortune to serve recognized Vaiṣṇavas.

King Kulaśekhara also gives us the vision of constant meditation on Lord Viṣṇu. This can be attained by engaging oneself twenty-four hours a day in various services within the framwork of the ninefold practices of *bhakti* (see *Śrīmad-Bhāgavatam* 7.5.24). A true Vaiṣṇava never thinks he has attained the ultimate state of perfection, but rather continues to serve the Lord and the devotees while always remaining conscious of the Supreme Lord in his heart.

TEXT 49

तत्त्वं प्रसीद भगवन्कुरु मय्यनाथे
विष्णो कृपां परमकारुणिकः खलु त्वम् ।
संसारसागरनिमग्नमनन्त दीन-
मुद्धर्तुमर्हसि हरे पुरुषोत्तमोऽसि ॥४९॥

tat tvaṁ prasīda bhagavan kuru mayy anāthe
viṣṇo kṛpāṁ parama-kāruṇikaḥ khalu tvam
saṁsāra-sāgara-nimagnam ananta dīnam
uddhartum arhasi hare puruṣottamo 'si

tat—therefore; *tvam*—You; *prasīda*—please show Your favor; *bhagavan*—O Supreme Lord; *kuru*—please give; *mayi*—to me; *anāthe*—who am without a master; *viṣṇo*—O Viṣṇu; *kṛpām*—mercy; *parama*—the most; *kāruṇikaḥ*—compassionate; *khalu*—after all; *tvam*—You; *saṁsāra*—of material existence; *sāgara*—in the ocean; *nimagnam*—submerged; *ananta*—O limitless one; *dīnam*—wretched; *uddhartum*—to lift up; *arhasi*—You should please; *hare*—O Hari; *puruṣa-uttamaḥ*—the Supreme Personality of Godhead; *asi*—You are.

TRANSLATION

O Supreme Lord, O Viṣṇu, You are the most compassionate. So now please show me Your favor and bestow Your mercy upon this helpless soul. O unlimited Lord, kindly uplift this wretch who is drowning in the ocean of material existence. O Lord Hari, You are the Supreme Personality of Godhead.

PURPORT

A complacent religionist may think a devotee need not call out for personal attention. "Lord Kṛṣṇa already knows everything, so there's no need for individual supplication." But according to the *ācāryas,* when a soul who feels himself helpless and unfortunate calls out to the Lord, he touches the Lord's heart. Śrīla Prabhupāda once gave an example of this while walking with his devotees in a park. A group of ducks in a pond swam forward toward the devotees, and the duck who quacked the loudest was given some food. Prabhupāda remarked that in a similar way we have to cry out for Kṛṣṇa, as a child cries for its mother. Of course this shouldn't be done in an egotistic or artificial way, but the Lord will respond to his devotees' sincere and helpless cries.

A devotee does not wish to bother the Lord with any demands or petitions, yet calling for mercy does not contradict the selfless mood of service. A good example is Gajendra, who asked the Lord to release him from the jaws of a crocodile. Śrīla Prabhupāda writes,

> Unalloyed devotees have nothing to ask from the Supreme Personality of Godhead, but Gajendra, the king of the elephants, was circumstantially asking for an immediate benediction because he had no other way to be rescued. Sometimes, when there is no alternative, a pure devotee, being fully dependent on the mercy of the Supreme Lord, prays for some benediction. But in such a prayer there is also regret. [*Bhāg.* 8.3.21, purport]

Queen Kuntī made a similar special request in her prayers:

> *atha viśveśa viśvātman viśva-mūrte svakeṣu me*
> *sneha-pāśam imaṁ chindhi dṛḍhaṁ pāṇḍuṣu vṛṣṇiṣu*

"O Lord of the universe, soul of the universe, O personality of the form of the universe, please, therefore, sever my tie of affection for my kinsmen, the Pāṇḍavas and the Vṛṣṇis" (*Bhāg.* 1.8.41). In these instances the pure devotees ask not for material benedictions but for the Lord to intervene and arrange things so that they may more fully surrender to Him. About Queen Kuntī's petition, Śrīla Prabhupāda writes,

> A pure devotee of the Lord is ashamed to ask anything in self-interest from the Lord. But the householders are sometimes obliged to ask favors from the Lord, being bound by the tie of family affection. Śrīmatī Kuntīdevī was conscious of this fact, and therefore she prayed to the Lord to cut off her affectionate ties for her own kinsmen, the Pāṇḍavas and the Vṛṣṇis. [*Bhāg.* 1.8.41, purport]

Also, there are many moving songs by Vaiṣṇavas of the recent age in which they call out to the Lord for individual help on the path of devotional service. For example, Śrīla Bhaktivinoda Ṭhākura sings in *Gopīnātha,*

> O Gopīnātha, this sinner, who is weeping and weeping, begs for an eternal place at Your divine feet. Please give him Your mercy.
>
> O Gopīnātha, You are able to do anything, and therefore You have the power to deliver all sinners. Who is there that is more of a sinner than myself?

Deeply considering his disqualifications and asking for special help, the devotee requests his savior to be compassionate. The devotee's recognition of his complete dependence on the Supreme Lord is a prerequisite for his purification. He knows that if Lord Hari does not respond, he has no one else to turn to.

King Kulaśekhara teaches us how to turn to Lord Kṛṣṇa at all times, whether in meditation while absorbed in His all-attractive name, form, and pastimes, or in desperation while sinking in the ocean of material life.

TEXT 50

क्षीरसागरतरङ्गशीकरा-
सारतारकितचारुमूर्तये ।
भोगिभोगशयनीयशायिने
माधवाय मधुविद्विषे नमः ॥५०॥

kṣīra-sāgara-taraṅga-śīkarā-
sāra-tārakita-cāru-mūrtaye
bhogi-bhoga-śayanīya-śāyine
mādhavāya madhu-vidviṣe namaḥ

kṣīra—of milk; *sāgara*—in the ocean; *taraṅga*—from the waves; *śīkara*—of the spray; *āsāra*—by the shower; *tārakita*—bespeckled; *cāru*—charming; *mūrtaye*—whose form; *bhogi*—the serpent's (Lord Ananta Śeṣa's); *bhoga*—of the body; *śayanīya*—on the couch; *śāyine*—who lies;

mādhavāya—to Lord Mādhava; *madhu-vidviṣe*—the antagonist of the demon Madhu; *namaḥ*—obeisances.

TRANSLATION

Obeisances to Lord Mādhava, enemy of the Madhu demon. His beautiful form, lying on the couch of the serpent Ananta, is speckled by the shower of spray from the milk ocean's waves.

PURPORT

This is a picturesque view of Kṣīrodakaśāyī Viṣṇu, the expansion of Lord Kṛṣṇa who inhabits the spiritual planet Śvetadvīpa. In the *Śrīmad-Bhāgavatam* (3.8.24) Śrīla Vyāsadeva also describes the beauty of Lord Viṣṇu as He lies in *yoga-nidrā:*

> The luster of the transcendental body of the Lord mocked the beauty of the coral mountain. The coral mountain is very beautifully dressed by the evening sky, but the yellow dress of the Lord mocked its beauty. There is gold in the summit of the mountain, but the Lord's helmet, bedecked with jewels, mocked it. The mountain's waterfalls, herbs, etc., with a panorama of flowers, seem like garlands, but the Lord's gigantic body, and His hands and legs, decorated with jewels, pearls, *tulasī* leaves, and flower garlands, mocked the scene on the mountain.

King Kulaśekhara describes Lord Viṣṇu as the killer of Madhu. Although in the form of Kṣīrodakaśāyī Viṣṇu the Lord did not kill Madhu, there is no contradiction in addressing the Supreme Lord by any of His pastime names. As Śrīla Kṛṣṇadāsa Kavirāja points out in his *Caitanya-caritāmṛta (Ādi* 5.128–130, 132),

> There is no difference between the incarnation and the source of all incarnations. Previously Lord Kṛṣṇa was regarded in the light of different principles by different people. Some said that Kṛṣṇa was directly Lord Nara-Nārāyaṇa, and some called Him Lord Vāmanadeva incarnate. Some called Lord Kṛṣṇa an incarnation of Lord Kṣīrodakaśāyī. All these names are true. . . . In whatever form one knows the Lord, one speaks of Him in that way. In this there is no falsity, since everything is possible in Kṛṣṇa.

The Kṣīrodakaśāyī form of Lord Viṣṇu is very rarely seen, even by advanced devotees. Sometimes when there is a crisis in universal management, Lord Brahmā goes to Śvetadvīpa to consult with Kṣīrodakaśāyī Viṣṇu. Brahmā sits on the bank of the milk ocean and chants the *Puruṣa-sūkta* prayers. In meditation, he then hears instructions from the Lord.

The shower of spray from the milk ocean speckling the Lord's form mocks the impersonal conception of the Absolute Truth. The source of all incarnations is not an impersonal effulgence but the transcendental Lord Himself, the Supreme Person. King Kulaśekhara does not manufacture images but strictly follows the Vedic descriptions of the Lord of Śvetadvīpa.

TEXT 51

अलमलमलमेका प्राणिनां पातकानां
निरसनविषये या कृष्ण कृष्णेति वाणी ।
यदि भवति मुकुन्दे भक्तिरानन्दसान्द्रा
करतलकलिता सा मोक्षसाम्राज्यलक्ष्मीः ॥५१॥

alam alam alam ekā prāṇināṁ pātakānāṁ
nirasana-viṣaye yā kṛṣṇa kṛṣṇeti vāṇī
yadi bhavati mukunde bhaktir ānanda-sāndrā
karatala-kalitā sā mokṣa-sāmrājya-lakṣmīḥ

alam alam alam—enough, enough, enough; *ekā*—by itself; *prāṇinām*—of living beings; *pātakānām*—of the sins; *nirasana*—driving away; *viṣaye*—in the matter of; *yā*—which; *kṛṣṇa kṛṣṇa*—"Kṛṣṇa, Kṛṣṇa"; *iti*—thus; *vāṇī*—words; *yadi*—if; *bhavati*—there is; *mukunde*—for Lord Mukunda; *bhaktiḥ*—devotion; *ānanda*—with ecstasy; *sāndrā*—dense; *kara-tala*—in the palms of one's hands; *kalitāḥ*—available; *sā*—she (devotion); *mokṣa*—liberation; *sāmrājya*—influence; *lakṣmīḥ*—and opulence.

TRANSLATION

By themselves the words "Kṛṣṇa, Kṛṣṇa" are sufficient to drive

away the sins of all living beings. Anyone who possesses devotion for Lord Mukunda that is densely imbued with ecstasy holds in the palms of his hands the gifts of liberation, worldly influence, and wealth.

PURPORT

King Kulaśekhara's declaration that the holy name drives away sins brings to mind a similar statement spoken by Nāmācārya Haridāsa Ṭhākura. First he quoted a verse that makes use of the analogy of the rising sun:

aṁhaḥ saṁharad akhilaṁ
sakṛd udayād eva sakala-lokasya
taranir iva timira-jaladhiṁ
jayati jagan-maṅgalaṁ harer nāma

"As the rising sun immediately dissipates all the world's darkness, which is deep like an ocean, so the holy name of Lord Hari, if chanted once without offenses, dissipates all the reactions of a living being's sinful life. All glories to that holy name of the Lord, which is auspicious for the entire world" (Cc. *Antya* 3.181).

Next Haridāsa Ṭhākura explained the verse as follows: As the first glimpse of sunlight dissipates one's fear of thieves and ghosts, so with the first hint of offenseless chanting of the Lord's names, reactions of sinful life immediately disappear. If a devotee can continue to chant without offenses, he goes on to awaken ecstatic love for Kṛṣṇa.

Then Haridāsa Ṭhākura stated, "Liberation is the insignificant result derived from a glimpse of the awakening of offenseless chanting of the holy name." When Haridāsa made this claim, a ritualistic *bhāhmaṇa* challenged him, saying that he had exaggerated the powers of the holy name. But Haridāsa Ṭhākura replied with śāstric proof. He gave the example of Ajāmila, who chanted the Lord's holy name with the intention of calling his son Nārāyaṇa, yet who was thereby immediately freed of his sinful reactions and who ultimately attained to the spiritual world. Haridāsa also quoted a verse from the *Śrīmad-Bhagavatam* proving that pure devotees prefer serving the Lord to being liberated without such service.

Śrīla Bhaktvinoda Ṭhākura elaborately describes the stages of chanting the holy name in his *Hari-nāma-cintāmaṇi:* Chanting that is full of ignorance and offenses is known as *nāma-aparādha.* The next stage, which still contains imperfections, is known as *nāma-ābhāsa,* or the shadow of the holy name. This is the stage in which one can attain freedom from sins and even liberation. But one can atttain pure *kṛṣṇa-prema* only by chanting without offense, a stage known as *śuddha-nāma,* or the pure chanting of the holy name.

King Kulaśekhara says that one who has attained love of Kṛṣṇa has all other benedictions easily within his grip, including *mukti* and the gifts of Lakṣmī, the goddess of fortune. The *bhakta's* indifference toward liberation is further expressed by Bilvamaṅgala Ṭhākura in his *Śrī Kṛṣṇa-karṇāmṛta* (107):

bhaktis tvayi sthiratarā bhagavan yadi syād
daivena naḥ phalati divya-kiśora-mūrtiḥ
muktiḥ svayaṁ mukulitāñjali sevate 'smān
dharmārtha-kāma-gatayaḥ samaya-pratīkṣāḥ

"My dear Lord, if I am engaged in firm devotional service unto You, then I can very easily perceive Your transcendental youthful form. And as far as liberation is concerned, she stands at my door with folded hands, waiting to serve me, and all material conveniences of religiosity, economic development, and sense gratification stand with her."

A pure devotee easily attains wealth and liberation, but he is not interested in them. As Śrīla Prabodhānanda Sarasvatī writes in his *Śrī Caitanya-candrāmṛta* (5), "[For a pure devotee] impersonal liberation is as palatable as going to hell, and the heavenly cities of the demigods are as real as flowers imagined to float in the sky." The devotee is *ātmārāma,* self-satisfied, because he knows that devotional service to Kṛṣṇa brings everything.

TEXT 52

यस्य प्रियौ श्रुतिधरौ कविलोकवीरौ
मित्रौ द्विजन्मवरपद्मशरावभूताम् ।
तेनाम्बुजाक्षचरणाम्बुजषट्पदेन
राज्ञा कृता कृतिरियं कुलशेखरेण ॥५२॥

yasya priyau śruti-dharau kavi-loka-vīrau
mitrau dvi-janma-vara-padma-śarāv abhūtām
tenāmbujākṣa-caraṇāmbuja-ṣaṭ-padena
rājñā kṛtā kṛtir iyaṁ kulaśekhareṇa

yasya—whose; *priyau*—beloved; *śruti-dharau*—expert in knowledge of the *Vedas; kavi*—of poets; *loka*—in the society; *vīrau*—eminent leaders; *mitrau*—two friends; *dvi-janma*—of the *brāhmaṇas; vara*—superior; *padma*—of the lotus; *śarau*—stems; *abhūtām*—have become; *tena*—by him; *ambuja-akṣa*—of the lotus-eyed Lord; *caraṇa-ambuja*—at the lotus feet; *ṣaṭ-padena*—by the bee; *rājñā*—by the king; *kṛtā*—made; *kṛtiḥ*—composition; *iyam*—this; *kulaśekhareṇa*—by Kulaśekhara.

TRANSLATION

This work was composed by King Kulaśekhara, a bee at the lotus feet of the lotus-eyed Lord. The king's two beloved friends are the twin stems of the exquisite lotus of the *brāhmaṇa* community, expert Vedic scholars renowned as leaders of the community of poets.

PURPORT

Like a bee at the lotus feet of Lord Kṛṣṇa, King Kulaśekhara has made honey in the form of his exquisite poetry, which overflows with nectarean descriptions of the Supreme Lord. He has also cried out to the Lord for deliverance from the ocean of material suffering. By using a wide repertoire of metaphors, and by speaking from the depth of sincere Vaiṣṇava feelings, he has made his readers indebted to him. Now they may also become bees and drink the honey of the *Mukunda-mālā-stotra.*

Among the twenty-six qualities of a devotee, one is that he is a *kavi,* or poet. The subject of a devotee's chanting and hearing comprises the superexcellent name, form, qualities, and pastimes of Kṛṣṇa. The qualified *kavi* receives Kṛṣṇa consciousness faithfully in *paramparā* and renders it into excellent poems and discourses. Thus it is said of the *Śrīmad-Bhagavatam* that "it emanated from the lips of Śrī Śukadeva Gosvāmī. Therefore this fruit [of the desire tree of Vedic literature] has become even more tasteful, although its nectarean juice was already relishable for all, including liberated souls" (*Bhāg.* 1.1.3). Describing the contribution of Śukadeva Gosvāmī to the *Bhāgavatam,* Prabhupāda writes, "The Vedic fruit which is mature and ripe in knowledge is spoken through the lips of Śrī Śukadeva Gosvāmī, who is compared to the parrot not for his ability to recite the *Bhāgavatam* exactly as he heard it from his learned father, but for his ability to present the work in a manner that would appeal to all classes of men." Like Śukadeva, King Kulaśekhara has imbibed the Vedic conclusions and added to them his own taste of devotional mellows.

In his *Govinda-līlāmṛta,* Śrī Kṛṣṇadāsa Kavirāja ends each chapter of his work with a statement similar to King Kulaśekhara's here. He writes, *śrī-caitanya-padāravinda-madhupa-śrī-rūpa-sevā-phale:* "This book is the ripened fruit of my service to Śrīla Rūpa Gosvāmī, who is a bumblebee relishing honey at the lotus feet of Śrī Caitanya Mahāprabhu."

The honey-sweet nectarean *rasa* of Kṛṣṇa consciousness is also expressed by Bilvamaṅgala Ṭhākura in his *Śrī Kṛṣṇa-karṇāmṛta* (92):

madhuraṁ madhuraṁ vapur asya vibhor
madhuraṁ madhuraṁ vadanaṁ madhuram
madhu-gandhi mṛdu-smitam etad aho
madhuraṁ madhuraṁ madhuraṁ madhuram

"This transcendental body of Kṛṣṇa is very sweet, and His face is even sweeter. But His soft smile, which has the fragrance of honey, is sweeter still."

TEXT 53

मुकुन्दमालां पठतां नराणां
अशेषसौख्यं लभते न कः स्वित् ।
समस्तपापक्षयमेत्य देही
प्रयाति विष्णोः परमं पदं तत् ॥५३॥

mukunda-mālāṁ paṭhatāṁ narāṇāṁ
aśeṣa-saukhyaṁ labhate na kaḥ svit
samasta-pāpa-kṣayam etya dehī
prayāti viṣṇoḥ paramaṁ padaṁ tat

mukunda-mālām—this flower garland for Lord Mukunda; *paṭhatām*—who recite; *narāṇām*—among persons; *aśeṣa*—complete; *saukhyam*—happiness; *labhate na*—does not achieve; *kaḥ svit*—who at all; *samasta*—of all; *pāpa*—sins; *kṣayam*—the eradication; *etya*—obtaining; *dehī*—an embodied being; *prayāti*—proceeds; *viṣṇoḥ*—of Lord Viṣṇu; *paramam*—supreme; *padam*—to the abode; *tat*—that.

TRANSLATION

Who among those who recite this *Mukunda-mālā* will not achieve complete happiness? An embodied being who chants these prayers will have all his sinful reactions eradicated and proceed straight to the supreme abode of Lord Viṣṇu.

PURPORT

Following the śāstric tradition, King Kulaśekhara ends his poem with an auspicious benediction for his readers. We find many such benedictions in the *Śrīmad-Bhagavatam*. For example, Canto Seven contains this statement: "Anyone who with great attention hears this narration concerning the activities of Prahlāda Mahārāja, the killing of Hiraṇyakaśipu, and the activities of the Supreme Personality of Godhead, Nṛsiṁhadeva, surely reaches the spiritual world, where there is no anxiety" (*Bhāg.* 7.10.47).

The Vaiṣṇava poet's blessing upon the reader is not merely a literary form. The *Śrīmad-Bhagavatam* or the *Mukunda-mālā-stotra* can deliver full benedictions to any receptive reader and send him back home, back to Godhead. One need only consider the elevated topics King Kulaśekhara has covered in his poem. For example, he has often mentioned that the holy names of the Lord can save us from *saṁsāra.* And he has exhorted us to call out to Lord Kṛṣṇa for protection. Indeed, the *Mukunda-mālā-stotra* is filled with friendly advice to chant Kṛṣṇa's names, bow down before Him, and serve Him with all our senses and mind. King Kulaśekhara has advised us to become a servant of the servant of the servant of the servant of the servant of the servant of the servant of the Lord. All these statements are actually injunctions directly from the Supreme Personality of Godhead and the *śāstras.* King Kulaśekhara has repeated them in his own voice and with his own convictions, but his prayers have the authority of the Supreme Lord behind them.

His Divine Grace A. C. Bhaktivedanta Swami Prabhupāda chose these potent verses for rendering as *The Prayers of King Kulaśekhara.* He began translating them into English for wide distribution through his magazine, *Back to Godhead.* It will be our good fortune to go on hearing these verses in earnest, to sing them repeatedly, and to study and remember them. As followers of Śrīla Prabhupāda, we will be particularly inclined to remember Text 33:

kṛṣṇa tvadīya-pada-paṅkaja-pañjarāntam
adyaiva me viśatu mānasa-rāja-haṁsaḥ
prāṇa-prayāṇa-samaye kapha-vāta-pittaiḥ
kaṇṭhāvarodhana-vidhau smaraṇaṁ kutas te

"O Lord Kṛṣṇa, at this moment let the royal swan of my mind enter the tangled stems of the lotus of Your feet. How will it be possible for me to remember You at the time of death, when my throat will be choked up with mucus, bile, and air?"

Appendixes

His Divine Grace
A. C. Bhaktivedanta Swami Prabhupāda

His Divine Grace A. C. Bhaktivedanta Swami Prabhupāda appeared in this world in 1896 in Calcutta, India. He first met his spiritual master, Śrīla Bhaktisiddhānta Sarasvatī Gosvāmī, in Calcutta in 1922. Bhaktisiddhānta Sarasvatī, a prominent religious scholar and the founder of sixty-four Gauḍīya Maṭhas (Vedic institutes) in India, liked this educated young man and convinced him to dedicate his life to teaching Vedic knowledge. Śrīla Prabhupāda became his student and, in 1933, his formally initiated disciple.

At their first meeting Śrīla Bhaktisiddhānta Sarasvatī requested Śrīla Prabhupāda to broadcast Vedic knowledge in English. In the years that followed, Śrīla Prabhupāda wrote a commentary on the *Bhagavad-gītā,* assisted the Gauḍīya Maṭha in its work, and, in 1944, started *Back to Godhead,* an English fortnightly magazine. Single-handedly, Śrīla Prabhupāda edited it, typed the manuscripts, checked the proofs, and even distributed the individual copies. The magazine is now being continued by his disciples in the West.

In 1950 Śrīla Prabhupāda retired from married life, adopting the *vānaprastha* (retired) order to devote more time to his studies and writing. He traveled to the holy city of Vṛndāvana, where he lived in humble circumstances in the historic temple of Rādhā-Dāmodara. There he engaged for several years in deep study and writing. He accepted the renounced order of life (*sannyāsa*) in 1959. At Rādhā-Dāmodara, Śrīla Prabhupāda began work on his life's masterpiece: a multivolume commentated translation of the eighteen-thousand-verse *Śrīmad-Bhagavatam* (*Bhāgavata Purāṇa*). He also wrote *Easy Journey to Other Planets.*

After publishing three volumes of the *Bhāgavatam,* Śrīla Prabhupāda came to the United States, in September 1965, to fulfill the mission of his spiritual master. Subsequently, His Divine Grace wrote more than fifty volumes of authoritative commentated translations and summary studies of the philosophical and religious classics of India.

When he first arrived by freighter in New York City, Śrīla Prabhupāda was practically penniless. Only after almost a year of great difficulty did he establish the International Society for Krishna Consciousness, in July of 1966. Before he passed away on November 14, 1977, he had guided the Society and seen it grow to a worldwide confederation of more than one hundred *āśramas,* schools, temples, and farm communities.

In 1972 His Divine Grace introduced the Vedic system of primary and secondary education in the West by founding the *gurukula* school in Dallas, Texas. Since then his disciples have established similar schools throughout the United States and the rest of the world.

Śrīla Prabhupāda also inspired the construction of several large international cultural centers in India. The center at Śrīdhāma Māyāpur is the site for a planned spiritual city, an ambitious project for which construction will extend over many years to come. In Vṛndāvana are the magnificent Kṛṣṇa-Balarāma Temple and International Guesthouse, *gurukula* school, and Śrīla Prabhupāda Memorial and Museum. There is also a major cultural and educational center in Bombay. Major centers are planned in Delhi and in a dozen other important locations on the Indian subcontinent.

Śrīla Prabhupāda's most significant contribution, however, is his books. Highly respected by scholars for their authority, depth, and clarity, they are used as textbooks in numerous college courses. His writings have been translated into over fifty languages. The Bhaktivedanta Book Trust, established in 1972 to publish the works of His Divine Grace, has thus become the world's largest publisher of books in the field of Indian religion and philosophy.

In just twelve years, despite his advanced age, Śrīla Prabhupāda circled the globe fourteen times on lecture tours that took him to six continents. Yet this vigorous schedule did not slow his prolific literary output. His writings constitute a veritable library of Vedic philosophy, religion, literature, and culture.

References

The purports of *Mukunda-mālā-stotra* are all confirmed by standard Vedic authorities. The following authentic scriptures are cited in this volume. For specific page references, consult the general index.

Ādi Purāṇa

Bhagavad-gītā

Brahma-saṁhitā

Bṛhad-bhāgavatāmṛta

Caitanya-caritāmṛta

Hari-bhakti-sudhodaya

Īśopaniṣad

Kali-santaraṇa Upaniṣad

Kṛṣṇa, the Supreme Personality of Godhead

Kṛṣṇa-karṇāmṛta

Mahābhārata

Matchless Gift

Mukunda-mālā-stotra

Nārada-pañcarātra

Nectar of Devotion

Nectar of Instruction

Padma Purāṇa

Padyāvalī

Śaraṇāgati

Śikṣāṣṭaka

Śrīmad-Bhāgavatam

Stotra-ratna

Śvetāśvatara Upaniṣad

Teachings of Queen Kuntī

Upadeśāmṛta

Sanskrit Pronunciation Guide

The system of transliteration used in this book conforms to a system that scholars have accepted to indicate the pronunciation of each sound in the Sanskrit language.

The short vowel **a** is pronounced like the **u** in b**u**t, long **ā** like the **a** in f**a**r. Short **i** is pronounced as in p**i**n, long **ī** as in p**i**que, short **u** as in p**u**ll, and long **ū** as in r**u**le. The vowel **ḷ** is pronounced like **lree,** **ṛ** like the **ri** in **ri**m, **e** like the **ey** in th**ey**, **o** like the **o** in g**o,** **ai** like the **ai** in **ai**sle, and **au** like the **ow** in h**ow**. The *anusvāra* (**ṁ**) is pronounced like the **n** in the French word *bo***n**, and *visarga* (**ḥ**) is pronounced as a final **h** sound. At the end of a couplet, **aḥ** is pronounced **aha**, and **iḥ** is pronounced **ihi**.

The guttural consonants—**k, kh, g, gh,** and **ṅ**—are pronounced from the throat in much the same manner as in English. **K** is pronounced as in **k**ite, **kh** as in Ec**kh**art, **g** as in **g**ive, **gh** as in di**g h**ard, and **ṅ** as in si**ng.**

The palatal consonants—**c, ch, j, jh,** and **ñ**—are pronounced with the tongue touching the firm ridge behind the teeth. **C** is pronounced as in **ch**air, **ch** as in staun**ch-h**eart, **j** as in **j**oy, **jh** as in he**dgeh**og, and **ñ** as in ca**ny**on.

The cerebral consonants—**ṭ, ṭh, ḍ, ḍh,** and **ṇ**—are pronounced with the tip of the tongue turned up and drawn back against the dome of the palate. **Ṭ** is pronounced as in **t**ub, **ṭh** as in ligh**t-h**eart, **ḍ** as in **d**ove, **ḍh** as in re**d-h**ot, and **ṇ** as in **n**ut. The dental consonants—**t, th, d, dh,** and **n**—are pronounced in the same manner as the cerebrals, but with the forepart of the tongue against the teeth.

The labial consonants—**p, ph, b, bh,** and **m**—are pronounced with the lips. **P** is pronounced as in **p**ine, **ph** as in u**ph**ill, **b** as in **b**ird, **bh** as in ru**b-h**ard, and **m** as in **m**other.

The semivowels—**y, r, l,** and **v**—are pronounced as in **y**es, **r**un, **l**ight, and **v**ine respectively. The sibilants—**ś, ṣ,** and **s**—are pronounced, respectively, as in the German word **s***prechen* and the English words **sh**ine and **s**un. The letter **h** is pronounced as in **h**ome.

Index of Sanskrit Verses

This index constitutes a complete listing of the first lines of each of the Sanskrit poetry verses of the *Mukunda-mālā-stotra,* arranged in English alphabetical order.

Index

Boldface page numbers indicate references to translations of verses of the *Mukunda-mālā-stotra.*